SURVIVING HARD TIMES

French-Canadian Weavers, Boott Mill, 1905
(Lowell Museum)

SURVIVING HARD TIMES

The Working People of Lowell

Mary H. Blewett
Editor

LOWELL MUSEUM
Lowell, Massachusetts
1982

To the people of Lowell.

CONTENTS

ILLUSTRATIONS

PREFACE

The story of the working people of Lowell is long overdue. It has been neglected for many years because it was an area of our city's history that was considered by many to be too controversial or a part of one's life best forgotten. When I was a student at Lowell State College, for example, I asked an elderly family friend to help me with my oral history course by sitting down and talking to me about her life in Lowell. She spoke freely of her reasons for coming to the United States from Greece, her work in the textile mills, and her family life and neighborhood. But, when I inquired about her involvement in labor activity, she hesitated and asked, "Why would you care about such things? It's over with." I was amazed that someone could just disregard a part of their lives as easily as that. Other students faced the same problems and continued to ask questions. The result was a series of research papers and interviews which documented, for the first time, the labor activities of textile workers in Lowell from 1875 to 1940.

The book focuses on the attempts by workers to improve themselves; to overcome bigotry and prejudice; to survive hard times. Much of the material is controversial, but every effort has been made to use documented accounts or the words of the participants themselves to tell the story. If Lowell is to celebrate its designation as a National Park dedicated to the working people of America, then the issue of labor and its activities must be explored.

Surviving Hard Times is the culmination of a great deal of work by a number of individuals ranging from the University of Lowell students who allowed us to publish their work to the members of the editorial committee who worked out the final draft for publication. No one, however, put in the countless hours that Dr. Mary H. Blewett of the University of Lowell did. Her work on this project began in 1973 when, as a pioneer in using Lowell as a teaching tool in the college classroom, she encouraged and worked with her students to research various aspects of the city's history with a primary focus on labor activity and social conditions. Within the past ten months, Dr. Blewett has volunteered her time and expertise to organize the material into a cohesive, readable format with the help of the editorial committee. She has contributed a great deal to the interpretation of Lowell's history, and for this she receives my personal and professional admiration.

Once Mary Blewett's support was enlisted, the question of financing the publication became crucial. The Lowell Museum is indebted to the members of the Lowell Historic Preservation Commission, U.S. Department of the Interior who offered through their Cultural Grants Program the monies which served as a basis for the production of this book. Additional funds were granted by the Lowell Historical Society, the Lowell Jaycees Housing Corporation, and University of Lowell Alumni Association. A special thanks to Wang Laboratories, Inc. which through its staff, Marilynn Bever, Alice Broderick, David Gallagher and Mabel Kelley, provided technical assistance in the publication process.

Finally, when all is said and done, the typing of the countless revisions and drafts is the responsibility of one person who tries to figure out the lines, the scribbles and the arrows. To Colette Lyons, we all offer our sincerest thanks for a job well done.

Surviving Hard Times is a reality, and the Museum is proud to have published it. There is, of course, more to be written and researched. Perhaps this will provide the basis for that work to be done.

Lewis T. Karabatsos
Director
Winter, 1981   Lowell Museum

INTRODUCTION

Mary H. Blewett

The intensive study of the lives and experiences of people in one community like Lowell is part of what modern historians call history written "from the bottom up." This is history interested in the culture and the working habits of the people. In the early Seventies, undergraduate history students at Lowell State College (the University of Lowell since 1976) began to study the history of the working people of Lowell. The post-Civil War period, virtually unexamined by historians, became the focus of their efforts. They wrote seminar papers based on research conducted in newspapers and city documents. They interviewed people; they compiled and wrote the history of their families. This group of essays represents a selection of this work; many other papers are deposited in the Special Collections at the Lydon Library of the University of Lowell. The papers were edited, and the footnotes were removed for the general readership of this book. The original papers with their complete documentation are available in the Special Collections.

Historians have always been interested in the pre-1860 period in the history of Lowell: the "Golden Age" of the building of the canals and mills, the miracles of industrial growth, and the legendary Lowell mill girls. Recent excellent examples of the analysis of this period include Thomas Bender, *Toward an Urban Vision* (1975), John Kasson, *Civilizing the Machine* (1976), and Thomas Dublin, *Women At Work* (1979). Even before the Civil War began, however, the city struck out in new directions. The first immigrants, the Irish, became mill operatives, replacing the rural Yankee women and adding cultural diversity to the neighborhoods and workrooms of Lowell. After the Irish had settled, the French-Canadians, the Poles, the Greeks, the Portuguese, Italians and many others followed. These major changes in the composition of the work force heralded what historian Herbert Gutman regards as the main theme of labor history in America: the successive waves of pre-industrial people confronting the industrial system.

A tradition of labor militancy established itself early in the Lowell mills when Yankee mill girls organized "turnouts" or strikes over wage cuts in 1834 and 1836. In the 1840s the Lowell Female Labor Reform Association, under the leadership of Sarah G. Bagley, became the first important labor organization for women. Bagley and other women activists organized female workers in several New England textile cities and testified before the Massachusetts state legislature in 1845 in favor of limiting the working day to ten hours.

What would be the relationship between the immigrant workers and this tradition of labor militancy? Would immigrant labor remain divided and passive? The answer came even before 1860 in a little noticed strike of female Irish throstle spinners. This strike of Irish women in 1859 forecast one of the major obstacles of the labor movement in Lowell: ethnic division. For ironically in 1859, the Yankee female operatives who had provided the backbone of labor militancy in the 1830s and 1840s now served as strikebreakers. Nevertheless, as these papers indicate, the tradition of labor militancy in Lowell would be carried on and reshaped by the new waves of industrial workers.

The first major example of post-Civil War labor activity is explored by Carol Polizotti Webb. In 1875 the mule spinners, a highly skilled group of workers of Irish and English backgrounds, struggled for higher wages. The outcome of the strike suggested that the organization of a single craft, vulnerable to the introduction of new machinery, was a poor basis on which to organize. In 1875 mill managers in Lowell worked together effectively to develop anti-union strategies which they would use over and over: the lockout, the blacklist, and the yellow-dog contract. Violence by strikers, frustrated over the power of managers to bring in strikebreakers and adapt spinning machinery to new work, weakened public sympathy for the mule spinners. The avoidance of violence in strikes became one of the cardinal principles of union activity in Lowell. The failure of a single craft to protect its interests led to the organization of federations of crafts among skilled workers which preceded the strike of 1903. The 1903 strike would test the use of a craft federation as an effective organizational base among textile workers.

The unskilled, whom the craft unions ignored, toiled at their low paid, low status mill jobs, surrounded especially in the Depression of the Nineties by various examples of the fate of those who failed to hang on to their places in the industrial system. Steve Allen, Kathy Gawlik and I studied what might be called the politics of misery. Allen analyzed the social phenomenon of the tramp whose ranks were swelled by the unemployed, created by the severe economic depression from 1893-1897. Depressions such as in the 1890s and the 1930s often forced idle workers to move about in a vain search for work. Public opinion refused to distinguish between the tramp who voluntarily chose a life on the road and the unemployed vagrant who desperately searched for the means to stay alive. The reaction of the people of Lowell to these tramps and vagrants was fear and revulsion. Rejection and harrassment became the fate of those unwilling or unable to find a steady job in the mills.

Gawlik and I examined municipal policy toward poverty as another way of demonstrating the community's attitude toward work. In Lowell there was no safety net for the poor. City officials responsible for poor relief feared that unearned aid of any kind was addictive to the recipient and dangerous to the community. The Lowell City Farm was maintained as a refuge of last resort for the desperate. The result was a policy which punished the victims of poverty. Again, the lesson was plain: without work a person had no status in the community. The city's policy of denying decent support to the hapless poor, however, was surely one of the many reasons why the various immigrant cultures in Lowell created voluntary, self-help organizations. As the 1903 and 1912 strikes demonstrate, these ethnic networks of relief and assistance proved valuable when workers were out on strike.

Municipal policy toward the poor separated the "worthy" poor from the "unworthy" poor in assigning relief of any kind. To city officials, all strikers who had voluntarily left their jobs were by definition unworthy. Ignoring the implications of these attitudes, the skilled workers of Lowell, who had status and could command the highest wages, conducted an important strike in 1903. One of the major issues in this strike was the role of unskilled, immigrant workers. Would these groups cooperate with the craft unions or, as management hoped, refuse to support the strike and remain at work? Shirley Zebroski's analysis of the strike contradicts the local suspicion that the Greeks, the Poles, and the Portuguese among others acted as strikebreakers in the Lowell mills. The second issue of the strike was the viability of the craft federation to represent textile workers. The strike of 1903 demonstrated that although unskilled workers were loyal to the strike, the Textile Council of skilled workers failed to reflect their interests or communicate effectively with them. When, prodded by hunger and destitution, the unskilled workers returned to work, management shrewdly offered to teach them the jobs abandoned by the craft workers and then blacklisted those remaining out on strike. Aggressive management tactics, organized and led by William S. Southworth of the Massachusetts Mills, exposed the weaknesses of craft unions operating in a large labor pool of workers eager for better jobs.

One of the key groups in the 1903 strike was the rapidly growing community of Greeks, typical of the new wave of immigration from Southern and Eastern Europe in the 1890s. Labor historians in the 1970s have studied the interplay of culture and work in the formation of class consciousness. The Greek experience as depicted by Lewis Karabatsos and Dale Nyder shows how culture strengthened the unity of Greek workers. However, cultural unity could also divide ethnic groups against each other and even expose one nationality to misrepresentation and bigotry. Unity among mill workers from different homelands was a difficult organizational problem, solved only by the Industrial Workers of the World in the 1912 strike.

The profound sense of community among the Greeks did not mean they lacked labor militancy. Greek workers disliked participation in strikes because of the hostility directed against them by public opinion which regarded them as temperamental and potentially violent foreigners. They needed steady work to support their growing families, but as in the 1907 strike against the Bigelow Carpet Company, they also stoutly defended the economic justice of their need for higher wages. They rejected unfair treatment and stood together as countrymen against management. Greek workers often participated in collective action. This potential for solidarity with other workers was usually contradicted, however, by their willingness to subordinate their interests as workers to middle-class Greek leadership. In this sense, cultural unity remained more important to Greek workers than class unity.

The divisions among the skilled and unskilled immigrant workers which had proven disastrous in the 1903 strike were not repeated in the 1912 strike, as Mary Mulligan describes it. The Industrial Workers of the World, a radical worker organization fresh from a great victory in the woolen mills of Lawrence, was committed to real democracy among all workers and careful to provide representation for and consultation with all ethnic groups on strike in Lowell. Against this genuine commitment to worker solidarity, the tactics of management were ineffective. The IWW advisors to the strike of 1912 also tried scrupulously to avoid violence and the perceived threat of social revolution. The strikers' demands were essentially bread and butter wage issues, but also included new power for workers on the shop floor. Under direct and intense pressure from other New England textile interests, Lowell managers agreed to settle the strike in an effort to prevent the repetition of the success of IWW strategy throughout the region. The strike of 1912 was a clear demonstration of the potential of industrial unions for textile workers.

The industrial union, however, did not reappear in the Lowell mills until the late Thirties. The federal government persecuted the IWW for its opposition to World War I, jailing its leaders and destroying the organization. Instead, the tradition of craft unions reemerged by 1918 under the leadership of the United Textile Workers, affiliated with the American Federation of Labor. The UTW had strongly opposed the presence of the IWW in Lowell and traced its own roots back to the Textile Council in the 1903 strike. The UTW was careful, after the success of the 1912 strike, to appeal to workers of all levels of skill but, according to Edward Scollan, failed to provide aggressive leadership during the labor shortages of World War I. The UTW seemed content with its conservative vision of higher wages as the total solution for worker complaint. In a quick and uneventful strike in 1918, the union bargained away the right to strike for a meager wage increase. Not until the labor shortages and production boom of World War II would industrial unions for textile workers become established in Lowell.

By the early Twenties, mill after mill in Lowell began to close its doors in the great decline of the textile industry in the Northeast. As companies moved South or went out of business, empty mill space and unemployed workers attracted new industries to the city, among them shoe making, garment stitching, electronic assembly, and later, plastics. These companies were looking for cheap rent, cheap labor, and no unions. The city, desperate for new payrolls and new sources of taxes, seemed to welcome them. Former textile workers, such as Yvonne Hoar, found work in the shoe shops. As Edward Rocha found, the labor militancy which had characterized textile workers became vital to the organizers of a shoe workers' union in an important strike in 1933. The strike was marked by a violent confrontation between strikers and strike-breakers along Bridge Street and in Kearney Square. The fact that the city police protected and escorted the strikebreakers and that the mayor followed policies which favored the shoe shop owners created a situation of dangerous tension. A settlement, brokered by the Democratic governor, forestalled further troubles and brought a union to the shoe shops. The strike of 1933 indicated that munici-pal policy, as in 1875, still favored management's position.

Yvonne Hoar was just one of the thousands of women workers who made up 40% of the textile labor force in Lowell. Her reminis-cences of work and life recapture the mood of the city as the textile industry began to falter and decline in the early twentieth century: the dark, dismal corporation houses, the tensions among the ethnic groups, the fights on the Common, the overwhelming, deafening noise of the weave rooms at the Merrimack. Yvonne Hoar was a vital, "cocky" young woman, a "spitfire" to her floor boss. She ex-perienced years of suppressed outrage over the injustices inflicted on workers by the Merrimack management: the surveillance, the "patronage" or favoritism in jobs, the terrors of losing a chance to work especially during the Depression years of the 1930s, the reli-gious discrimination against Catholics, the ethnic snobbery aimed at "all us foreigners."

Yvonne Hoar worked at various jobs. She started at the Merri-mack in 1924 as a finisher of cotton velvet; during World War II she inspected bullets on a Remington Arms Company assembly line; she was a floor girl at the shoe shops and a spooler at the Wan-nalancit Mills. Ending her education at fourteen, she acquired her training on the job. She worked all her life and solved her need for child care in ways familiar to working-class mothers in Lowell. She watched the father, whom she loved and respected, work long hours, seven days a week as a machinist at the Merrimack. He con-nected textile machinery together to facilitate the "stretch-out," a means of assigning double and triple work for the same pay. He was anti-union, but Yvonne knew what the stretch-out meant to workers, and she had to defy her father to become a union organizer.

Her energy and sense of fairness and justice were tapped as the Merrimack workers began to organize in 1938. As historian Marc Miller has argued recently, women played an important but unpaid role as labor organizers in the textile mills. Without their support as participants in unions, the mills would never have been organized. Alice Swanton, a retired mill worker interviewed by Miller in 1975, remembered Yvonne Hoar's activities organizing the Merrimack before World War II. "Mrs. Hoar did it . . . . That woman took on the whole Merrimack, and she fought them to a standstill . . . . She had the heart of a Lion . . . . It was something to see that woman at a meeting [with management]." But Yvonne Hoar, as committed as she was to unionism, refused to force her female co-workers to join the union at the Merrimack, despite pressure from the union's business agent. Without a union contract that specified a closed shop, she would not substitute union coercion for management coercion. Nor could she forget the "poor souls" she saw, the unemployed during the Depression or those unjustly fired from their jobs or bilked by local merchants. Her good humor and forthright speech lighten the otherwise grim details of life around her.

James Ellis, a Greek-American born Boutselis in 1919, left Lowell High School at seventeen to work in the dyerooms of the Merrimack Mills, as many young Greeks had before him. There, in the midst of the steam and the sweat, he had an experience which impelled him into labor activity. Joining with others like Yvonne Hoar, Ellis channeled his anger over poor working conditions and harsh treatment of workers into organizing the Merrimack. The Merrimack Manufacturing Company had been the first mill built in Lowell and the first to produce cotton cloth from the water power of the Merrimack River during the city's Golden Age. It was also the first to be unionized.

Ellis soon found that his success as a young business agent for the union focused local opposition on him. He was fired, blacklisted, and labeled a Communist. He was drafted, in disregard of his draft status, and even while in the Army, he was persecuted for his allegiance to the Congress of Industrial Organizations (CIO). When Ellis left for active duty, his young replacement as business agent for the union at the Merrimack was also drafted. Leadership for the local union had to come from those ineligible for military service: older men and women like Yvonne Hoar. After the war, Ellis followed the textile industry to the South, working as an organizer for the CIO in the 1940s and 1950s. Compared with his experiences in Lowell, he faced a much more open and hostile resistance to labor unions in Southern mill towns.

"The Family History of Sophie and Theresa" spans almost the entire period of this book. Sophie was born in Poland around 1890; her husband, Stanley, was ten years older. Sophie immigrated to the United States around 1910, remarried and had two children by the time World War I broke out. The families of Sophie and Theresa were "poor souls," in Yvonne Hoar's words. They were unskilled, immigrant mill workers, and when the Depression hit, they lost their jobs. They experienced all of the miseries of poverty and the alienation and isolation of the immigrant. Poverty was corrosive to their lives; it produced bitter resentment, hatred, meanness, and brutality. They desperately clung to traditional ways, and to their children — especially their sons — for security. Their miseries were compounded by the devastating flood in 1936.

Once Sophie's son, Joe, was fifteen and able to work, he assumed sole responsibility for his family. In order to get a job, he walked five miles a day for a solid month to sit in the waiting room of a factory on Bridge Street to impress the boss with his desperation. Sophie's reaction to his eventual employment was a flood of gratitude: "They had let him work." Joe's desperate situation, however, soon led to exploitation, until he fought back against his employers. Memories of the Depression years were nightmares for both Sophie and Theresa. But better times came with World War II: more jobs, higher wages, the chance to own property, a house, a car, modern appliances. Family members intermarried with other ethnic groups but often faced hostility from the older generation. With their tiny share of post-war affluence, they traveled and sent their children to college. The meaning that they were able to find in the hard experiences of their lives seemed reflected in the ambition and success of their children and grandchildren.

After the decline of the textile industry and during the ensuing economic troubles which came to Lowell, many blamed "the unions" for the departure of the mills and the loss of wages and jobs. The evidence in these chapters on the labor history of the city does not sustain that traditional belief.

It is clear that the post-Civil War immigrant work force did carry on the labor activism begun by the Yankee mill girls. There was plenty of labor militancy and many strikes. There was, however, little institutional strength or continuity in union organizations.

Not until the late Thirties did the strategy of the industrial union take the shape of a real organization which linked itself nationally to the CIO. By then, much of the textile industry had left New England.

Elitism and disregard for the unskilled workers of recent immigration had blinded the earlier craft union leadership and limited its effectiveness. Shrewd, anti-union policy by mill managers and shop owners, jointly planned and aggressively carried out, undermined worker resistance by adopting new technology, dividing ethnic and skill groups, and utilizing local police powers to protect strikebreakers. Violence in strikes was usually assiduously avoided, but when management wielded power which seemed overwhelming, as in 1875, or unfair, as in 1933, resistance became immediate and physical.

In 1854 Charles Dickens, who had visited Lowell during its Golden Age in the 1840s, published his novel, *Hard Times*, which examines the impact of the factory system and the philosophy of utilitarianism on the British nation. Few of Dickens' characters in *Hard Times* escaped the total corruption of their lives by industrialization. In contrast, the working people of Lowell were survivors. This study of the major strikes in the history of the city, the general attitudes toward the unemployed and the poor, and a reconstruction of the tough experience of some of its citizens provides one way to recapture the lives of the working people of Lowell.

Many people worked on the preparation of *Surviving Hard Times*. The most important were the college students who researched the topics or conducted the interviews and who wrote the seminar papers. They deserve thanks for their generosity in allowing the publication of their efforts and for the patience with which they dealt with the efforts of the editor. The editorial committee: Lewis T. Karabatsos, Robert W. McLeod, Arthur L. Eno, Jr., Peter F. Blewett and Charles F. Carroll, asked searching questions and improved the quality of the writing. The editor is grateful for the time and energy that each person devoted to this endeavor. Special thanks go to Lew Karabatsos who carried the idea for a book like this around in his head for years and finally made it possible by raising the money. As a teacher and an historian, nothing could delight me more than its publication. However, this is only a beginning; there is much more to be discovered about the experiences of the working people of Lowell.

THE LOWELL MULE SPINNERS' STRIKE OF 1875

Carol Polizotti Webb

The Lowell mule spinners' strike of 1875 was part of the post-Civil War struggle to achieve effective craft union organization for skilled workers. The attempt to raise wages for these skilled workers in Lowell resulted in a decision by management to import strikebreakers and to try to utilize another technology to undercut the craft. Plagued by lack of a strike fund and unruly members, the mule spinners' union failed to match the united opposition and effective strategy of the mill agents. As a result, the mule spinners lost the strike in 1875.

Individual craft unions had begun to organize in the major New England textile centers as early as 1850. The first wave of European immigrants, the Irish, began to replace the Yankee women in the mills in the 1840s, and corporate paternalism which had marked the early years of Lowell had practically disappeared by 1850. The inexperience of immigrant labor, combined with their desperate need for work, made the Irish an attractive alternative to Yankee operatives who were beginning to organize collective protests against wage cuts and for the ten-hour day. When unions of experienced workers went out on strike, management replaced the strikers with those willing to work and to learn. High prices for raw cotton prompted management to lower labor costs by cutting wages between 1850 and 1870. Skilled workers, like the mule spinners, organized to oppose these wage cuts.

Mule spinning was a major process used in cotton and woolen cloth production until the 1890s. Throstle spinning had preceded mule spinning and had provided both warp and filling yarn suitable for the coarse cotton cloth which the Lowell mills had first produced. The process of mule spinning, in general use by the 1850s, involved a great deal of strength, required the supervision of assistants, called "back-boys," and was, therefore, considered men's work. Cotton fibers, already in the shape of a soft roll, called roving yarn, were stretched and twisted into thread by the mule spinning machine. Part of this very large machine moved in a track guided by the mule spinner who drove it back and forth, putting just the right amount of tension on the yarn to produce very fine filling thread for highly finished fabrics. Consequently, the operator of this machine had to be a highly skilled worker.

The introduction of ring spinning, a technology invented in 1828 but not perfected until 1871, caused problems for the mule spinners and would hasten their demise as a highly skilled craft. Ring spinning not only produced a coarser thread than mule spinning, more suitable for warp than for filling yarn, but it also involved much less skill on the part of the worker.

If the rings could spin thread adequate for filling, the male mule spinner could be replaced by a cheaper, female work force. The ring spinning machine, unlike the mule, was wholly stationary. The tension on the yarn which had been provided by the skilled operator was now determined by a series of weights. The mule spinner physically drove the mule along its track, thereby manually guiding the yarn as it was being spun. In the ring spinning machine, a small metal ring, or traveler, was attached to the bobbins on which the thread was wound. This small metal catch spun around rapidly and gave the thread extra twist while guiding it along the turning bobbin. The metal ring did the work of the skilled operator.

The organization of mule spinners into unions came earlier than that of any other textile trade. Most of the mule spinners in Lowell were of English or Irish birth, and they followed the English style of militant and vigorous labor agitation. The New England mule spinners' organizations, especially in Fall River, the center of labor activity, were modeled after the Lancashire textile unions in Great Britain. As a group the mule spinners were extremely proud of their skills and abhorred the thought of unskilled women taking over their domain. They remained reluctant to organize the ring spinners into their craft unions. They were also an extremely volatile group, quick to anger. Superintendents and agents regarded them as a troublesome lot and were eager to divide the spinners'

Cotton Mule Spinners (Merrimack Valley Textile Museum)

groups against each other. Thomas M. Young in *The American Cotton Industry* (1902) related this story:

> "The mule spinners," said one mill superintendent to me, "are a tough crowd to deal with. A few years ago they were giving trouble at this mill, so one Saturday afternoon, after they had gone home, we started right in and smashed up a roomful of mules with sledge-hammers. When the men came back on Monday morning, they were astonished to find there was no work for them. That room is now full of ring frames run by girls."

The struggle of the mule spinners in 1875 was not only to improve their wages, but to maintain their position in the structure of the textile industry. It seemed a fight for survival.

Lowell members of the mule spinners' union, who had organized a local in the 1850s, were strongly influenced by their counterparts in Fall River. Early in 1875, Fall River mule spinners had demanded a wage increase and protested the conversion of some spinning operations from mules to rings. The refusal of the mills to respond brought on a massive strike. In early April, increased communication between the two cities resulted in rumors of a strike in Lowell.

The Lowell strike began at the Lawrence Manufacturing Company on Monday, April 12, after a weekend organizational meeting with representatives of the striking mule spinners of Fall River. The next day the strike spread to the Massachusetts and Prescott Mills. By April 14 all union mule spinners were out on strike. The reaction of the corporations was to lock out all mule spinners, whether they were union members or not. This decision, however, deprived the mills of filling yarn for weaving operations and threatened to halt production. The strategy of the mill management throughout the strike was to devise a means of keeping production going and thereby destroy the local union. They meant to accomplish this in three ways: adapt ring spinning machinery to produce fine filling thread; use supervisory personnel and section hands to run the mules; and import strikebreakers from other textile centers. This was the strategy feared by the Fall River unions. A leading textile manufacturer in Fall River later congratulated the Lowell corporations on their unity and aggressive tactics.

The corporations' strategy, however, had its weak points. If the ring spinners could be organized, and the strikebreakers intimidated and forced to leave town, production of cotton cloth could not be kept going. On April 14 as the strike was spreading to the

Tremont and Suffolk, the Merrimack, the Boott, and the Appleton Mills, female ring spinners at the Hamilton Company left their work in a group to demand a wage increase. Small numbers of other ring spinners also struck several other corporations. They met on April 15 at Lynch's Hall on Market Street, the headquarters of the mule spinners' strike. During the meeting, representatives of women working as ring and throstle spinners at all the corporations passed the following resolutions:

> Resolved, That we, the ring and fly [throstle] spinners of Lowell, do pledge ourselves to demand an advance of pay immediately; and be it further resolved that we assist, to our utmost ability, the mule spinners in the pending struggle.

> Resolved, That we form a union as soon as possible to defend ourselves against all tyranny and oppression.

The ring spinners were organizing themselves. Back-boys, who served as assistants to the mule spinners, were another important group to keep out of the mills. On April 16 the first violence of the strike occurred between French-Canadian back-boys fighting among themselves over who was a strikebreaker.

The mule spinners' strike committee was hesitant, however, to get involved in the ring spinners' cause. Prospects for strike funds were limited and probably could not be extended to other groups. The mule spinners, as a group of craftsmen, would find it difficult to associate themselves with a less-skilled and less well-paid group of women workers. Nonetheless, the potential of cooperation by the ring spinners in the strike was recognized by the Fall River unions who sent Cassie O'Neill, a young weaver active in the Fall River strike, to Lowell to speak to a meeting on April 26 at Huntington Hall.

The meeting was opened by the mule spinners marching in a body from Market Street to Merrimack Street led by a brass band. The president of the Lowell union, John Butterworth, addressed a crowd estimated by reporters to be composed half of men and half of women. He extolled the importance of unity between working men and working women and catalogued the grievances of the mule spinners: wage cuts, speed-ups, and their inability to witness the weighing of the yarn for which they were paid by the pound. He acknowledged that other workers had similar grievances but did not propose immediate action for them. Other speakers denounced the corporations and pointed to wage increases recently won by mule spinners in Lawrence.

Portuguese Ring Spinner, Appleton Mills, c. 1910
(Lowell Historical Society)

When Cassie O'Neill spoke at the meeting, she promised that money from Fall River was on its way to the Lowell strikers and that more would come. She asked the working women of Lowell to unite and invited the female ring spinners to "knock at the door" of the mule spinners' union for admission. O'Neill encouraged women weavers and ring spinners to join the strike, form unions, and ask for wages equal to those of men. " 'In conclusion,' she said, 'let it not be said that the women are a dead weight to the mule spinners of Lowell.' "

However, instead of helping the ring spinners organize, the striking mule spinners concentrated their efforts on the strikebreakers, either by persuading them to join the strike or threatening them with harm. This was dangerous; violence could alienate public sympathy.

Management's strategy continued to unfold during the first week of the strike. While reorganizing their work force to keep cloth production going, the mills also put pressure on the mule spinners by blaming them for the shorter hours and reduced wages experienced by other workers, such as the weavers who were deprived of work by the lack of filling yarn. The corporations considered a general lockout which would deny employment to all textile workers. They circulated rumors that experienced female mule spinners from Salem were in town and ready to work. The *Daily Courier* worried about the impact of lagging production on the income of textile operatives on whom many local businesses depended for customers.

One day after the April 26 meeting of the strikers and their sympathizers at Huntington Hall, the corporations announced that they were all spinning filling yarn, either with ring spinning machines or with the help of strikebreakers from out of town. Some claimed production at 80% of normal, but regardless of the amount of yarn actually spun, it symbolized the corporations' defiance of the mule spinners' union.

On the night of April 27, the first serious violence involving mule spinners and the men they called "nobsticks" and "bummers" erupted. A shooting incident occurred on the Merrimack Street Bridge over the Suffolk Canal. One striker was slightly wounded. J. K. Chase, a night police officer at the Lawrence Company, and several watchmen, who were accompanying strikebreakers to their boarding houses, had witnessed a stoning incident at the corner of

Moody and Hanover Streets. The strikebreakers under attack proceeded to the Merrimack Street Bridge where a confrontation with a group of waiting strikers took place. Blows were exchanged, and a shot was fired. Both groups appeared to be armed, but a strikebreaker, David Kennedy, employed by the Lawrence Corporation, was arrested. A searing editorial in the *Daily Courier* appeared on April 28, condemning the incident:

> The discontented operatives on either side will gain no sympathy by an exhibition of violence. If we acknowledge the legal right of a mule spinner or any number of mule spinners to refuse to work at less wages than they think they ought to receive, and to combine in any lawful manner to secure what they want, it is also equally clear that any man who chooses to work for less has the right to do so without molestation or interference.

Although the incident on April 27 resulted in no serious injury, the agents of the mills took the opportunity to request the city government to set up a special police force to protect "the spinners now filling the place of those out on strike." By May 3 special police were on duty, lending the support of municipal tax money to management's strategy of bringing strikebreakers into Lowell to run the mules. On May 5 the agent of the Tremont and Suffolk announced that fifty-one ring spinning frames were producing filling yarn alongside of fourteen pairs of mule spinning machines. Production, he claimed, was 60% of normal, and he was looking for customers to buy the rest of his mules.

For a while, the mills' ability to continue to spin filling yarn was interrupted by a dispute with the section hands who were the foremen of the mule spinning rooms. Section hands were running the mules in the place of the strikers. Overworked and without adequate pay to compensate them for their risky position with the mule spinners, the section hands, although unaffiliated with the union, walked out of the mills on May 3. The disagreement was resolved two weeks later, and they returned and began once again to operate the mules.

Frustration over the ability of management to sustain production created severe tensions among the strikers. Efforts had been made by the strike committee to divert their energies into organized sports. Pledges against drinking during the strike were solemnly taken during meetings of the strikers. The parents of back-boys were urged to send them to school and keep them off the street and out of trouble. Still, ugly incidents began to happen. On April 24 the *Daily Courier* had reported that a man who had come to Lowell to work was:

> ... set upon by half a dozen of the strikers on Paige Street yesterday afternoon, and one of them gave him a severe blow in the mouth, knocking him down. Quite a crowd collected. The party assaulted said that he had been out of work all winter, and would run the risk of being pounded to death rather than to starve.

On May 10 striker Michael Grady was arrested for allegedly threatening "to put a bullet through" back-boy Edward Connelly, if the boy continued to work at the Hamilton. When furniture store dealer Jacob Nichols intervened to try to protect young Connelly, Grady socked him in the face. Grady was fined in Police Court and ordered to keep the peace.

Lack of financial support from other mule spinners' locals also weakened the strike. Some money arrived on May 4 from the mule spinners in Lewiston, Maine and New Bedford, Massachusetts, but the promises made by the Fall River union were never kept. After the strike ended, *The Fall River Labor Journal* revealed that the falling prices for cotton textiles in the late spring had persuaded the Fall River mule spinners that the strike in Lowell would fail. The editor also stressed the effectiveness of management strategy:

> If it had not been apparent to the spinners of other cities that the success of the manufacturers in procuring spinners to take the places of those on strike had substantially rendered it certain that the movement must fail, they might have responded more liberally to the calls for funds.

Representatives of the Lowell mule spinners traveled to other textile centers to plead for strike funds, but they returned with little more than pledges of support. As a result, there was no general distribution of funds to strikers. Back-boys, whose families depended on their wages, must have found it hard to stay out of the mills.

The first break in the ranks of the striking members of the Mule Spinners' Association occurred on May 2. Two strikers returned to work, one at the Lawrence and the other at the Merrimack. To get their jobs back, they had to sign "yellow-dog contracts." which made any association with a union grounds for dismissal. After the 1875 strike, the yellow-dog contract began to be used extensively by the corporations in Lowell and throughout New England. The next day, the strike committee signalled defeat by organizing a delegation of two striking mule spinners from each corporation to seek a compromise with the agents of the mills.

No meeting was ever held. Over a hundred mule spinners, expecting to be blacklisted, left the city. Only about fifty of the 227 striking mule spinners were eventually hired back. To return to work, they too had to sign a yellow-dog contract disavowing union activity. The strike ended officially on May 24, and the *Daily Courier* denounced the situation as:

> ... the supreme folly of men putting themselves under the control of a union which is managed by outsiders and without any intelligent appreciation of the situation . . . . They will hardly be so foolish again.

However, the mule spinners' union in Fall River remained viable and continued to try to organize locals in other textile cities. A recurrent pattern of lost strikes and blacklisted union members continually jeopardized the mule spinners' locals everywhere but Fall River. In the mills the proportion of ring spinning machines able to spin filling yarn grew each year after 1875, and this growth was stimulated in the 1890s by the introduction of the automatic loom which required stronger filling yarn. An effort was made to organize the ring spinners in Lowell in the 1890s, but by 1901 the craftsmen in mule spinning abandoned this strategy and looked instead to a new federation of skilled trade workers to protect their interests.

TRAMPS AND UNEMPLOYED VAGRANTS IN THE DEPRESSION OF THE NINETIES

Stephen Allen

There have always been men called tramps who roamed the countryside for the sheer pleasure of it and because life on the road limited their responsibilities. With only a pack on their back and complete freedom to choose their direction, these wanderers seemed to enjoy a romantic life of ease and abandon. They cared nothing about the availability of jobs because they had permanently rejected the settled life of obligation and routine. However, the severe economic depression which began in 1893 swelled the numbers of vagabond people with vagrant men and women who traveled in desperation, driven by unemployment, seeking work.

In the depression years of the 1890s the Lowell newspapers tried at first to separate the genuine tramp from the unemployed vagrant. The *Lowell Sun*, in an editorial on October 17, 1893, made the observation that:

> The men who go out daily to seek employment are not those who go to the overseers of the poor for help and then spend their time loafing around the streets or on the commons.

Distinctions between the two groups became increasingly difficult to make in a general economic depression. Both groups came to face the same problems of survival and the same attitudes from the community which classified them both as "tramps." Local observers reacted negatively to the existence of large numbers of tramps in the area and condemned them as a disgrace and a threat to Lowell.

   In the early months of the depression in the fall of 1893, the city
government became greatly concerned about the influx of unemployed men into the city. The main concern was the danger these
people represented to the community. The destitute condition of
the tramps was of secondary importance. Editorials in the *Lowell
Sun* in October 1893 especially reflected this attitude. The editorials
argued that tramps would first beg and, if unsuccessful, would
steal whatever they wanted or set buildings on fire. The *Sun* editors
believed that some work should be provided to the tramps so that
they could earn a meal. Otherwise, they would be a menace to the
community. On October 24 the *Sun* suggested that arrangements be
made by which the tramps and beggars who appeared at local
doors would be fed at the police station or some other place appointed by the city authorities. The *Sun* also supported relief work
on streets and sewers for the unemployed.

   In the fall of 1893 some work for the idle of Lowell was considered by the city, but the program never got past the planning stage.
Proposals for relief were considered by the city council on October
27, but councilors questioned whether people outside the city
would come to Lowell to obtain this work and take the jobs away
from the idled workers of the city. Most of the jobs were in the
Street Department, and some also feared that the two dollars a day
paid to the relief workers might influence the people earning one
dollar a day in the mills to quit and join the Street Department.

   The council also questioned a plan by the Protestant Church
League which proposed to open up its office on specific days to receive applications for employment and relief. Some councilors
feared any such step would bring to the city every idle worker
within twenty miles. The fear of an influx of tramps into Lowell
caused the council to abandon plans to give its own idled workers a
way of earning some money. Some aid in the form of food was
provided to the hungry by various private groups. One aid station,
run by a Captain Gardner, was actually a tramp's retreat and was
located in an old school house on Church Street opposite the First
Baptist Church.

   The community's image of tramps was that of a large group of
roving drunks and criminals, who begged what they could and
stole the rest. This attitude contributed to public uneasiness and
was promoted by a front-page story in the *Lowell Sun* on October
30, 1893, which said that Centralville was infested with tramps:

> Complaints are coming in thick and fast of the insolence and daring of a small army of tramps which seem to be closing in on Lowell. The gentlemen of leisure first made their appearance in numbers eight days ago and they seem to have come from all directions .... When they first began calling they were fed, but now that they are demanding cash instead of food, women are refusing and in return are being sworn at. Every morning from seven to eight o'clock, numerous gangs of tramps may be seen coming along the Poor Farm Road. They are tough-looking customers, and have the appearance of being tramps from choice and not necessity.

Despite the fears of the writer, the tramp population was primarily made up of individuals.

Generally speaking, the life of the tramp consisted of the constant problem of obtaining a meal and, if the tramp was traveling, a lot of walking. The tramp was a slave to the weather, especially during the winter months when all problems were magnified by the cold and snow in New England. Certain homes were well-known among tramps for their generosity; they knew what one might expect to receive at each house. In the summer of 1894 the *Lowell Evening Mail* carried a story concerning a tramp who asked for a meal at a residence in Ward Six, saying that he preferred cake. He claimed to be very hungry and was given a piece of fresh cream cake. Another tramp who had been treated well at the same house had put the tramps' cabalistic marks on the house so that others would know what kind of requests to make. These homes and their residents were lifesavers for many tramps.

When the weather permitted, usually from April to October, the tramps would roam from city to city. There was a circuit which was well-known among the tramps, especially those classified as professionals, and it encompassed many of the cities in the Merrimack Valley. For example, a tramp might travel from Haverhill to Lawrence to Lowell and on to Nashua to Manchester, New Hampshire; it appears many walked and, whenever possible, rode the rails. Upon completion of the circuit, they would return the same way. The Police Court records published in the newspapers provide much information about tramps and show a regular pattern and frequency of the same names in the various city court records. Many of the tramps who were arrested claimed residency in various cities. Upon arrest, often for drunkenness, the tramps were given a choice by the court of either leaving the city for their "home" or facing a fine or imprisonment. Obviously, many tramps took advantage of the option and said they would go "home." In reality, they would merely go on to the next city on the circuit, frequently being arrested again and thus continuing the pattern. For most tramps this pattern had a limit, forced upon them by the various municipal courts when their appearances became too frequent or their crimes more serious.

Not all the tramps who passed through Lowell in the Nineties were residents of the Merrimack Valley. Some came from New York, Connecticut and other New England states, while others came from as far away as Kansas City and Chicago. Hitchhiking was limited to a slow ride on a farm wagon. Some tramps traveled by rail when the train was heading in the right direction. A few tried to "borrow" a horse and wagon to lighten their burden; these tramps usually ended up by being arrested in the next town. Generally, the tramp was forced to walk most of his traveling miles to the next destination.

During the spring some tramps, especially the professionals, would leave Lowell. This was pointed out by the *Lowell Morning Times* of May 12, 1894:

> This is the season of the year when the tramp bestirs himself and selecting a few comrades, deserts the city and makes pilgrimages through the country.

The ones that stayed in the city were mostly those tramps who either had a desire or vague hope of obtaining some kind of employment or simply liked the comradeship.

In the warm weather, the tramps were more active, and they were much more in the public eye. Some of their activities consisted of just wandering around, gathering in groups, primarily on the South Common where they usually entertained themselves by playing cards and drinking. In fact, it appeared that drinking was by far the most popular pastime. It became the prime reason for trouble and resulted in many arrests for disturbing the peace. Fights broke out, as indicated in the *Lowell Evening Mail* of August 6, 1894:

> The South Common seemed to fairly swarm with bums and loafers all day. Friday and in the evening the condition of things was no better. [Various fights broke out and during an arrest, a police officer was assaulted by a tough named Frank Magee. Magee was caught and charged with assault and battery and sentenced to six months in jail.] But it is doubtful if this will induce the crowd to conduct itself any more decently in the future.

The newspapers reported that the Lowell police station entertained more out-of-town drunks than any other in the state, except Boston. Tramps would sleep on the Common or anywhere they could find a cool, comfortable plot of ground on which to rest. Sometimes complaints were filed against a sleeping tramp by someone offended by his presence. The punishment was often severe. An example of this was a complaint filed against Kate Foley, one of the few female tramps who comprised no more than 2% of the total tramp population. She was found sleeping in the rear of Hood's Laboratory on Thorndike Street and was arrested. She pleaded not guilty to the charge of leading the life of a vagrant but was sentenced to eight months at the State Farm. Generally speaking, however, problems were less acute for the tramp during the summer months, especially for the few who had obtained employment in one of the mills or on the city Street Department.

During the summer, some left the city for the countryside where life was less confining and the chances for arrest were fewer. There was also the opportunity or at least the hope of securing some temporary work at one of the many farms in the surrounding towns. The farmers appreciated the cheap labor, and room and board was no problem. The tramp, if he was allowed to stay, would sleep in the barn and eat food grown on the premises. One story which appeared in the *Lowell Morning Times* on June 26, 1894, described one arrangement in the city:

> A friend of mine allowed the grass on his lawn to grow nearly a foot tall during the warm days. He hadn't the courage to cut it. Saturday morning before 7 o'clock a sunburned tramp turned up at his house and offered to cut the hay. He would charge by the hour he said. The tramp got the contract and a sickle. At 12 o'clock the owner of the lawn returned to dinner and the tramp was just finishing the job. "It took me longer than expected," said the tramp, "and I will have to charge you 10 cents." "And you work by the hour?" asked my friend. "Ten cents for five hours work? Where do you come from?" "I'm from Pennsylvania," said the tramp. "I thought you didn't come from around here." said my friend, and he gave him a quarter. The tramp seemed to think he had struck a lump of luck.

But not all the tramps were humble and grateful, nor were all employers lucky to find honest and hardworking help. Joseph Emerson of Billerica was lucky to escape with his life when one of the hired tramp workers severely beat him.

As the summer progressed into the fall, the tramps had to make plans for the winter and the ones in the country headed into one of the cities. Many who were Merrimack Valley residents headed for their "home." The city had more benefits for the tramp in the winter, and chances of obtaining temporary work were better. Also, the tramps needed to stick together to help reduce the loneliness which many felt. No longer could a tramp sleep outdoors. Some kind of work was necessary to help the tramp survive, and no longer was it a matter of choice.

The city policy of allowing tramps to lodge at the police station upon request helped the tramps survive the winter. A few were more selective about their choice of a place to sleep, as described by the *Lowell Sun* on December 22, 1893:

> A Belvidere lady who found a tramp asleep in her kitchen yesterday forenoon was no more surprised than the tramp himself was upon awakening from his sleep, in a cell at the police station, whither he had been gently hustled into the patrol wagon.

The police station lodging policy at least reduced the chance of a tramp catching pneumonia or freezing to death. The number of lodgers at the police station was reported on a monthly basis. There were lodgers year-round, and of course, their number increased greatly as the weather grew colder. In July 1894 there were 161 lodgers, two of them female. In January of the same year, the number was 868. The *Lowell Sun* of January 12, 1894, illustrated this:

> "Tramps hotel" in the police station was crowded last night. It had 40 guests, including every kind of tramp known . . . . A professional tramp always carries his bed with him and last night's crowd were all professionals. The bed consists of a large piece of wrapping paper the thicker the better not necessarily clean, which is spread carefully on the hotel floor. [Coats were used as pillows.] Last night the tramps told many stories of their experiences . . . . This morning, they were treated to palatable crackers and digestible water.

Some tramps were lucky enough to find work. A few obtained work at one of the various factories. The most fortunate were those who were hired by the city on a temporary basis to shovel snow off the streets and trolley tracks. The pay was generally a dollar a day, which helped, but it didn't snow every day, and the tramp had to eat. Some would beg and call on those residents who had been charitable in the past. Some of the beggars met with little sympathy, as the *Lowell Sun* on January 18, 1894, relates:

> Tramp — Please mum, I ain't had a full stomach in three weeks. Housekeeper (Benevolently) — Too bad! Well, you can go somewhere and beg a meal of dried apples, and I will furnish the water.

Those unable to find work became desperate, and some tried to drink their problems away. Others turned to stealing food, clothes or money:

> Residents of Ward 5 are up in arms at the frequent depredations by tramps, who go begging from house to house. The men travel in pairs and call at the front doors, and if they are not given handouts, steal anything they can lay their hands on.

One typical "sneak thief" who was begging for food called on a local family. The tramp, William Sullivan of Troy, New York, stopped at a house and asked for food. Upon leaving, he took an overcoat off a hanger in the hallway and proceeded out the door. The house was owned by police officer Frank Fox, who was at home and saw Sullivan leave with the coat. Sullivan, who was arrested and appeared in court the following day, was sentenced to one month at the State Farm. Another tramp, even more daring and apparently more desperate, was reported to have walked off with a half of a hog from the doorway of a butcher on Market Street.

Many of these people had no hope except to be arrested and sentenced to the State Farm where there was at least a period of assured food and some warmth. Because lodging in the police station was only temporary relief, it provided little food; crackers and water appeared to be the typical meal, and conditions were barely liveable. Arrest was their only hope. However, the *Lowell Sun* on January 12, 1894, pointed out the weakness of this policy:

> The overseers of the poor would do the city a signal service if they would provide some means of affording tramps an opportunity of earning a mere subsistence. When a man goes up to a police officer and asks to be arrested, that he may escape starvation, there is danger to the community.

Two particular cases in the winter of 1894 emphasize the plight of these men:

> William Noonan of Fall River said to the court: "I ain't the worst sort of fellow, your Honor. I can turn my hand to anything." It was learned Noonan had no home or friends and the court sent him to the Farm for the four winter months.

A boy by the name of James Myers was also charged with vagrancy. His mother was dead, and he hadn't seen his father in three years. He made a living during the warm weather shining shoes, but in winter, he had no work and no home, so he asked the court to send him away to some school until the warm weather returned He was sent to the Reform School at the City Farm for five months.

Tramp arrests were more often for drunkenness than for vagrancy. During the period from July 1894 to February 1895, cases of vagrancy increased as the depression worsened. Charges such as wandering the streets or being a suspicious person were also lodged against people who looked like tramps. Still, even with the increase of vagrancy arrests, very rarely were more than ten people a month arrested for that offense. Charges other than these, such as assault and petty larcency, appeared to be rare, when compared with the total number of tramps arrested for drunkenness.

The defendants usually appeared in Police Court the day following their arrest. The court was presided over by Judge Samuel P. Hadley. Defendants appeared and a statement of their case was read, followed by their plea. Sentencing was left up to the discretion of the judge. Hadley presided regularly, and he knew many of the people who appeared before him, especially since most were charged with drunkenness and many for repeated offenses. The sentence for drunkenness varied from the option of leaving town, in the case of a tramp, up to as much as six months at the State Farm for local residents. Hadley took the defendant's personality and attitude into account, and the result was a wide disparity in his sentences. Six months was the maximum.

Vagrancy cases were different. Usually Judge Hadley was confronted with a stranger. He had little knowledge of his personal background, and this along with the general attitude and fear of tramps and vagrants made sentencing stiffer and less variable in these cases. A few were given the option of leaving town, but most were sentenced from six to eight months at the State Farm. A few others got off with just two months. The general attitude toward tramps usually took the form of fear or disgust and a conviction to rid the city of the supposed tramp menace. For example, one editorial in the *Lowell Sun* on December 18, 1894, stated:

> Was the Saturday night fire incendiary? If so an effort should be made to catch the firebug. Common loafers, vagrants, tramps, sons of rest and idle or suspicious characters of all kinds should be kept under the closest vigilance by the police.

But there were cases where a certain amount of affectionate regard was shown toward a few. One of Lowell's most famous tramps was

Lowell Slim, whose autograph was said to be on every freight car in New England. Another tramp, George Farrin, was a dwarf and served as the mascot for the local baseball team for a short time during his stay in Lowell.

Most tramps of the Nineties, whether they were genuine vagabonds or the unemployed, were feared because of the image which the newspapers and local opinion had of them — roving bands of idle criminals, begging and stealing whatever they could get their hands on. If they stole, they were hungry and desperate. City authorities offered them a choice of jail with crackers and water or the City Poor Farm. Most tramps grouped together not for crime but out of a need for companionship. They more often than not took whatever work might be available to them in these years of economic hardship. Those unskilled workers who managed to hang on to their jobs in the textile mills of Lowell during the hard times of the Nineties watched what happened to the "tramps" and remained quiet.

THE POOR AND THE CITY FARM: MUNICIPAL ATTITUDES TOWARD POVERTY

Mary H. Blewett

In the late nineteenth and early twentieth centuries the city of Lowell maintained an institution for the poor called the City Farm located on Chelmsford Street. At the City Farm the poor of Lowell were housed and granted aid. Relief was also administered to other poor people living outside the City Farm premises. While poverty is difficult to study through official records prepared by salaried administrators, the Reports of the Board of the Overseers of the Poor and the City Farm reveal the attitudes of city officials toward the poor.

During the period under study, poverty was regarded, in almost all cases, as inexcusable. Most middle-class Americans believed that hard work alone led to individual success. This idea was so central to American thinking in the late nineteenth century that the poor were themselves blamed for their condition. It was not society's fault if they could not properly support themselves. The problem was the individual; he or she was lazy or intemperate. Even the depression years of 1893-1897 did not alter these official attitudes. Municipal policy toward the poor made sure that there was no escape from the humiliation and degradation of poverty. The poor, including the sick, the aged, the insane, and children of paupers or criminals were all considered as misfits and placed together, at the lowest possible cost, at the City Farm.

Public policy toward the poor vacillated between minimal charity and total callousness. Sharing public tax money with those regarded as unwilling to work violated the doctrine that hard work brought success. The city distinguished between the "worthy" poor and the "unworthy" poor. Relief given at the City Farm conformed to these definitions. Very few were regarded as worthy. Those found starving who had not applied for aid because of pride were considered the most deserving. They received some temporary "outdoor" relief, a food order at a local store or some wood or coal. A man who had lost his job temporarily, but who was expected to be self-supporting soon would be granted relief if it were his *first* request for aid. A second request would condemn him to the list of unworthy poor. During the depression of the 1890s, the Secretary of the Board of the Overseers of the Poor, Martin J. Courtney (whose brother William served as mayor of Lowell from 1893 to 1895) described the dangers of giving too much aid to a worthy person. "In times of depression, not only old liners, but new ones who have never been aided before, get into the habit of being supported. That habit, when once cultivated, is hard to rid them of."

A third category of poverty cases, the insane, children of paupers and criminals, the sick and the elderly were usually classified as "unfortunates." Yet subtle hostility was directed toward them by municipal authorities. Courtney described them as a "burden" on the city, and he made strenuous efforts to minimize the expense of their care and housing. The indigent elderly were spared the designation of unworthy, but the Overseers of the Poor placed great emphasis on the need to teach the younger poor thrifty habits so that they could provide for themselves in their old age. Children were regarded as the most deserving group among the poor; however, genetic inheritance was regarded as one of the causes of poverty. Children might be "the innocent victims of the sins of others," but on the other hand, city officials believed they would become the next generation on the relief lists. In 1897 Courtney viewed heredity as one of the five primary causes of pauperism, and argued bitterly that much relief went to a class of:

> ... intemperate and worthless men and women, whose only ambition in life is gastronomic and bibulous in its tendencies, who not only feed themselves from the public crib, but propagate paupers for future generations.

The Board of Overseers of the Poor labeled the unworthy poor as lazy or intemperate. During the depression years of the 1890s their attack on the unworthy poor intensified, despite widespread unemployment and misery among the jobless. The public listing of the names of paupers was intended to be shameful and humiliating, but in 1895 Courtney, referring to the unworthy poor, wrote that it is "no concern to them if their names are on the pauper rolls. They glory in it." In his report for 1897, Courtney lists his five primary causes of pauperism: intemperance, inheritance, shiftlessness, lack of employment and sickness. Illness was the most tolerated category, although the sick person was not always thought to be worthy. The Secretary opposed giving aid to people who were unemployed. Lack of employment, he said:

> ... serves as a cloak for the unworthy .... The evil of pauperism flourishes and becomes a nauseating ulcer on the body politic; and this species of the "genus bum" is so common and persistent that the cause of the worthy is irreparably damaged.

During the depression years, Courtney feared the growing expense of poor relief and attempted to use the unworthy poor as a scapegoat for holding poor relief to a minimum. From 1893-1897 only 747 people were added to the pauper rolls, and municipal spending on the poor for the same period increased by only $3500.

Courtney's attitudes toward the poor and his complete control as Secretary of the Board over deciding who would receive aid at all city agencies involved in poor relief must have been a great deterrent to all but the most desperate. In Courtney's words, the Secretary:

> ... is held personally responsible for the aid rendered, both indoor and outdoor cases, and must look after the condition of each case that is under the control of the Board. Coupled with this are the duties of establishing and hunting up all claims for settlement, the disposition of the sick and insane, and the placing out of children.

An article in the *Lowell Sun* on January 2, 1901, told the story of a pregnant mother of two children, in desperate need of aid, having only a half loaf of dried bread for supper. Deserted by her husband and too ill to work, the woman described Courtney's contact with her as follows:

> They are talking of taking me to the City Farm until my child is born and of taking my two little boys to the day nursery. I can't bear to part with my children, it would seem like tearing my heart out .... I do so hate to have them separate me from my children. My rent is $2 a week, and I can easily get along with $2 for living expenses.

She had been found at home unconscious for seven hours, suffering from "lack of medical treatment." A collection had been taken up for her at the Hamilton Mills, where she had been employed, to pay her back rent, and a grocer on Central Street supplied her with food. The woman did eventually go to the City Farm, where she gave birth to a child, and died.

In order to apply for any type of outdoor relief, an application had to be filed with the Secretary of the Board of the Overseers of the Poor. A complete investigation followed. If the Secretary accepted persons for aid, their name, address and the amount of cash or value of provisions would be entered on the pauper register. The names can still be found in the City Auditor's Report for each year. Cash allowances were frowned on by the Board as an inappropriate way of giving aid. Cash, it was believed, was not always used for the intended purpose. Orders for provisions were preferred. All wood and coal provisions were delivered directly from the City Farm to recipients of aid.

Three blind men worked at the woodyard on the City Farm. They did all of the sawing and splitting of wood, thereby keeping themselves and their families off the pauper rolls. A superintendent was in charge of the yard, and two teamsters were employed to deliver the wood and the coal. However, city departments also purchased wood from the City Farm at a considerable saving to the taxpayers. Courtney claimed that the practice enabled the city to "purchase large quantities of wood and coal at wholesale prices, thus saving the middleman's profit."

Other types of relief provided by the Board were: burial of paupers, payments to state hospitals for the treatment of the insane, payments to institutions and hospitals for care of the sick, a horse-drawn ambulance service, and a City Dispensary and six physicians, one located in each of the city's six Wards. All applications for aid were first approved by Courtney, and orders were then given to the Ward physicians approving their visit to the homes. If, in the opinion of the Secretary, "recipients are worthy, medicine is furnished upon prescriptions of outside doctors." So doctors could not visit patients until they were deemed worthy sick persons by the Secretary. The filing of the application, the investigation and approval, and the wait for the physician must have taken at least a day. The Dispensary, located in City Hall, provided a place where those not bed-ridden could go for medical treatment.

In 1895 Courtney estimated that, despite his efforts, at least 40% of the outdoor aid given by his department went to unworthy people. However, he believed that pauperism could not be stamped out entirely because it was an inevitable part of industrial life:

> Lowell's class of inhabitants necessarily make her the foremost pauper city in the state, and on that account, we should be the foremost in our methods of contending with the evil.

Courtney regarded mill operatives as inevitably headed for poor relief unless he prevented it. His main concern as Secretary was to cut his expenditures. Courtney offered no program during the depression to aid the city's poor. The remedy, in his opinion, was hard work; the lack of jobs, however, was not his concern. "Employment is the enemy of pauperism." Courtney believed that every able-bodied applicant, worthy or otherwise, should be compelled to do some labor for what he received. The city could not have found an administrator more able to keep relief costs at a minimum. His contempt for the poor under his care allowed him to follow a policy of giving the least amount of aid possible to the smallest number of people.

The end of the depression years did not soften Courtney's attitude toward the needy. In 1902 he emphasized the need for constant surveillance of those granted temporary outdoor relief. "When the unworthy know they are being watched, they will be more wary of seeking aid." He advocated "using the pruning knife" to cut cash allowances and proposed a rule that would have a person declared a vagrant and criminally liable if he made application for admittance to the City Farm too often.

Courtney was more extreme in his condemnation of the poor than other Secretaries of the Board. His basic views on poverty, however, were held by many others in Lowell, including the Ministry-at-Large, a charitable, non-denominational religious organization. The Ministry-at-Large recommended instruction in thrift for the poor: that is, teaching people how to manage what they had, even though it was insufficient. When they were happy with what they had, they would be taught to have pride in "honest" poverty. The Ministry did, however, recommend the establishment of free kindergartens in Lowell, a reform that, had it been adopted, would have been of great benefit to working-class mothers.

The City Farm where the poor were maintained and housed was generally referred to as the "Poor Farm," but it was not a refuge for the poor alone. Other inhabitants of the Farm were the insane, male and female prisoners of the Municipal Jail, those committed to the Reform School, the chronically ill, children of paupers and prisoners, and sometimes tramps. The City Farm was basically a community of misfits, whom the city had deemed it necessary and economical to house together. It was cheaper to bring these different groups of people together into a city-controlled institution than it was to support them in private institutions.

By transferring the chronically insane from state hospitals to the City Farm, Lowell saved $1.36 a week per inmate in 1895. Any city of 50,000 or more inhabitants was permitted by state law to maintain an insane asylum. No person, however, could be classified as chronically insane until his insanity had continued for one year. Any person insane for less than a year and, therefore, not chronic had to receive treatment in one of the state insane asylums. At the end of one year, any patient who could, in the opinion of the superintendent of the state hospital, be taken care of at the City Farm would be transferred there. Although a physician made daily visits, the City Farm was staffed only by attendants. Without proper medical care, the insane lost all chance of recovery when they were transferred to the City Farm.

The prisoners from the Municipal Jail proved of great value to the Farm. They were sentenced by the Municipal Court to the Farm workhouse, and the city derived the benefit of their labor. According to City Farm Superintendent Lorenzo Phelps in 1880, "if they were sentenced to the House of Correction, the city could get no compensation for their support." The prisoners cultivated the garden crops which were then consumed at the Farm, delivered to outdoor aid recipients, or sold at market prices.

Young boys and girls, committed to the Reform School by the Municipal Court, came in handy in the summertime working on the Farm. Boys from neighboring cities and towns were sentenced to the Lowell Reform School at less cost than needed to maintain them in local facilities. Lowell could charge their communities for their support, and the City Farm got the value of their labor. The cost of supporting children in asylums outside of the City Farm or in private families was $1.25 per week per child. Children over four years of age could not, by law, be kept in a pauper institution, but the Nursery at the Farm did house children under four.

According to the *Lowell Sun* in 1901, no institution in the city provided a home for orphans under two years old, and "the only thing to do with a helpless little one is to make a pauper of it, and carry it to the City Farm." The children at the Farm had daily contact with prisoners and paupers until 1902 when the Nursery was moved to the cottage once occupied by the Chaplain. The Chaplain, a Protestant, held services twice daily, morning and evening prayer. Occasionally mass was said by one of the Catholic priests in the city.

John J. Donovan, Lowell's first Irish mayor, elected in 1882, constructed two new buildings at the City Farm. The Insane and Pauper Buildings were built in 1883 at a cost of $60,000; they were built of brick, heated by steam and equipped with fire escapes. The insane had not been housed at the Farm before 1880. The Board of Overseers of the Poor had decided at that time to bring the chronically insane back to the City Farm from the state hospitals. In an address in 1884, Mayor Donovan supported this decision and announced that he would petition the state legislature to grant Lowell a license to house the insane. This would enable the judge of the Police Court to commit people directly rather than send them to Danvers for a year, then be discharged, and returned to Lowell. The petition was never filed, but its intent was clear. The city could be saved the additional cost paid to state institutions during the one-year treatment period when the insane had not yet been classified as incurable.

The original buildings at the Farm, described in 1880 as "old and ill-contrived," were regarded as dangerous firetraps by Superintendent Phelps, but the old buildings were not torn down when the new buildings were finished in 1883, because the new buildings were still not large enough to accommodate all the inmates of the Farm. The two oldest buildings, condemned in 1880 by the superintendent, were used to house children, those sentenced to the Reform School and inmates of the Nursery. The number of buildings at the City Farm was always inadequate for the number of inhabitants of various types. The Insane Building housed the chronically ill and the insane, while the Pauper Building contained both paupers and prisoners.

To put poor people, most of whom were quite elderly, in the same building as younger prisoners served only to increase the horror and shame of the poor. Poverty was openly equated with crime. The Reform School contained both juveniles committed for minor offenses and children over the age of four who were waiting to be transferred to other institutions, a mix not condusive to reformation. Placing physically ill and mentally unstable people together invited danger. A deranged patient could easily harm an invalid. Conversely, living with old, dying people was not helpful for mental patients. The expenditure of money needed to separate inappropriate groupings was, however, seen as a greater evil.

A detailed description of the buildings at the Farm allows insight into the interaction between the groups and the conditions under which they lived. The main portion of the Insane Building was partitioned into two separate sections. The front portion was occupied by women and the back by men. Two dining rooms were located in the basement. Bath tubs and iron sinks were placed in hall passageways. The closed ward, where "dangerous lunatics" were confined, was located on the first floor in a large room with side bedrooms. On the second floor was an open ward for the feeble-minded with rows of cots on one side and bedrooms on the other side. This open ward led to an adjoining room which was the hospital ward. Those considered harmlessly insane were, therefore, in direct contact with the chronically ill. It is no wonder that the poor of Lowell chose to die at home in their beds. Courtney related a story in 1903 of one such woman:

> The scene I found there beggars description. She was wrapped up in several quilts, in a dirty bed and within a few hours of her death. Not a trace of a fire was there and the house had not been cleaned up for many a day. She was head-strong and stubborn and resented all friendly overtures from her neighbors. Hospitals or the City Farm were places of terror to her and it was only by promising to take her to one of her relatives that I gained her consent to go in the ambulance. She died in less than twelve hours after we moved her.

In the basement of the wing of the Insane Building was the washroom, the bakery and the kitchen. Here food was prepared for all of the inmates of the Farm and delivered by carrying it through the open air in pails. Separate food was prepared in another kitchen for the superintendents. The Pauper Building was also divided by sex. Elderly married couples, if they chose to be City Farm inmates, were separated from each other even at meals. The dining rooms for the inmates were located in the basement. The dining room, sitting room, and kitchen for the officials of the institution were on the first floor.

City Poor Farm, c. 1890 (Lowell Museum)

The second floor contained the bedrooms for the paupers. On the third floor were the prisoners' bedrooms. There were bars on their windows, but no locks on the doors of any bedrooms. The door leading to the third floor was locked at 8:00 p.m. The building provided little separation between the pauper and the prisoner. During the day, the prisoners worked in the gardens or around the buildings. They shared an exercise yard with the insane until 1894 and came into frequent contact with the Reform School children.

The total number of youngsters committed to the Reform School during a typical year (1893) was sixty. Of this number, thirty-nine were Lowell residents and twenty-one were from other cities and towns. Two-thirds were committed for truancy from school, the rest for larceny, vagrancy, "wandering about the streets," and other petty crimes. Two were committed for being neglected by others, and a third for being "stubborn." Over two-thirds were native-born Americans; the rest were foreign-born. One-third of the children were in the Reform School for a second, third or fourth time. Along with them were orphans or abandoned children. The average age of the Reform School inmates was twelve, of the orphans, ten. The latter included neglected children sent to the Reform School by the Municipal Court. They occupied the same quarters and attended the same classroom as did the juveniles committed to the Reform School under sentence. Little distinction was made between the two groups. The Nursery was occupied by children under four years of age who had been committed by the Board because their parents were either in jail or unwilling or unable to support them. On their fourth birthday, they went to the Reform School.

During these years, especially the hard times of the Nineties, the city of Lowell neglected to care for the needs of the poor. The poor living outside the Farm were given very little. Those living at the City Farm were huddled together and forgotten. The insane, whom the city had wanted to care for locally to save money, lived in deplorable conditions. The Insane Building was infested with rats. The hospital had to be disinfected regularly, and the patients moved into tents. Improvements were made on the buildings at the City Farm, but they never kept pace with the needs. It took twelve years, from 1883 to 1895, for the city to separate some of the insane from the ill, and when improvements were made, they were not totally effective. A large increase in the number of inmates at the Farm by 1901 did not result in additional staff; the inmates were compelled to do the work of attendants. The city shoved all of its unwanted citizens out of sight into an obscure institution and deprived them of the care that they might have received elsewhere.

The city authorities responsible for the poor wished to blame poverty on the choices made by its victims. Who would choose poverty over wealth? Poverty brought hunger, despair and the City Farm. Shaped by municipal policy, the City Farm became a symbol of the deprivation and failure which awaited those who failed the test of individual success. The image of the City Farm was a projection of the fears of the community about idleness and poverty. The depression years intensified these fears, but even then there was no excuse for poverty in the view of city authorities. The Board of Overseers of the Poor seemed intentionally to keep the City Farm in a condition which positively discouraged the poor from seeking aid.

THE 1903 STRIKE
IN THE
LOWELL COTTON MILLS

Shirley Zebroski

Labor organization has undergone many changes in the twentieth century as craft unions have given way to industrial unions.
When craft organization was at its peak, whole industries could be
crippled by a strike of skilled workers, but this did not last. With
technological advances, unskilled immigrant labor replaced union
craftsmen. Management was also willing to train immigrants so
that they could take over skilled positions. Management regained
control over labor by utilizing its right to hire and fire, reduce
wages, lock out workers, and employ easily managed, immigrant
labor. In order for labor to obtain power, craft unions had to be su-
perceded by a new industrial unionism, which included both
skilled and unskilled workers. The Lowell cotton textile unions,
however, confronted this situation only after a devastatingly unsuccessful strike. The Lowell strike of 1903 is an example of the
ineffectiveness of craft unionism in a changing industrial system.

By the 1840s the Irish began replacing the Yankees and British as
textile workers. After the Civil War the French-Canadians and
later, Southern and Eastern Europeans moved into the mills. By
1900 Yankees and Irish workers occupied most of the skilled positions, while the later-arriving immigrants entered the unskilled
and lowest-paid mill jobs. The New England mills depended on
these new immigrants because the native-born labor force had left
many of the unskilled positions to seek better paying jobs. The
owners welcomed this new labor force because they believed it

could be easily manipulated. In case of labor struggles, certain immigrant groups would be used as strikebreakers and, therefore, help to destroy any union solidarity in the textile industry.

The textile operatives worked long hours and received low pay. In 1900 the average hourly wage was ten cents, while in all other manufacturing industries, the average wage was twenty-one cents an hour. At no time between 1900 and 1926 did the earnings of cotton mill workers approach the average for all other industries. In 1903 the average weekly hours in all manufacturing industries was fifty-seven, but in the cotton mills, it was sixty-two hours. On a yearly basis the cotton workers made considerably less than other industries, because they were generally unemployed for several weeks. This occurred when poor market conditions made it unprofitable for the mills to run full-time. The cotton mill worker could expect to work only nine months out of the year, and a few more weeks if he were lucky.

In order to subsist on poor wages and unstable employment, the whole family was obliged to work. On the average the male head of the family earned 54% of the family income, the children 29% and the wife 7%, the rest came from other sources. Sometimes the whole family would be employed in the same mill. Under these circumstances, there were many young women in the mills, and they were generally in the least-skilled and lowest-paid jobs. Some 45% of all operatives in 1900 were women. Management preferred them to men because they were regarded as more reliable, cheaper, more industrious, faster, neater, more careful, and less likely to organize and strike.

The textile industry was very difficult to organize into unions because of the heterogeneous make-up of the operatives. The workers were divided by nationality, religion, sex, and skill. However, some unionization did emerge. The first skilled craft to organize was that of the mule spinners. Despite the blacklisting of workers after lost strikes and the growing use of ring spinning machines in the mills, the mule spinners kept an organization alive in Fall River. The union in Fall River then successively organized a series of locals in other textile cities. By 1901, however, efforts to extend the union to include the ring spinners were abandoned in favor of a craft federation — the United Textile Workers of America — which represented among the spinners only those who operated mules.

Some additional union organization took place in the skilled departments of the weavers, followed by the card room operatives, the slashers, and the loom-fixers. All these craft unions offered strike and death benefits. By 1900 there were five national craft unions with most of their strength centered outside of Lowell in Fall River and New Bedford. They were organized loosely along national lines and maintained strong local autonomy. Of these unions the mule spinners and loom-fixers were the best organized. All five unions were generally separated from the rest of the mill operatives by skill and nationality.

The American Federation of Labor (AFL) had given a charter to the mule spinners in 1893 and worked toward an amalgamation of scattered craft unions in the textile industry. In 1896 the AFL founded the Industrial Union of Textile Workers but reorganized it in 1901 when the leadership strayed too far to the left on social issues. The union was renamed the United Textile Workers of America (UTW) and embraced most of the organized skilled workers of the cotton industry in New England. The UTW leadership was closely watched by the AFL to see that it maintained a conservative outlook. The union was for skilled operatives only and was concerned primarily with economic gains in wages and hours.

The UTW faced many problems at the turn of the century, because the local crafts wanted to maintain low per capita payments to the national union and control their own treasuries. The individual unions preferred to help only those workers within their own craft. As a result of these problems, the UTW had difficulty during hard times assessing all its unions which represented various crafts. There was much factionalism in UTW unions, and the membership in the national union fluctuated from year to year; in 1903 there were 11,000 UTW members.

In Lowell, craft unions had organized local skilled workers. These skilled operatives represented only a small percentage of the mill population, perhaps only 10%. These unions were represented by the Lowell Textile Council which as a federation helped coordinate the activities of the craft locals. Its president was Robert Conroy of the Beamers' Union, and its fifty-six members represented the unions of the carders, weavers, beamers, mule spinners, loom-fixers, knappers, and knitters.

The members of these unions were predominantly Irish-American, with a scattering of French-Canadians. Most of the unorganized and unskilled mill workers were French-Canadians, Poles, Portuguese and Greeks. At this time 90% of the mill workers in Lowell were immigrants, and two-thirds of the laboring population in Lowell were employed in the textile or machinist trades. In 1900 only 20,000 out of the 94,000 residents of Lowell, or 21%, were of native birth.

Not only did the skilled workers organize, but the mill management had also organized. Each cotton mill named an agent to confer with the other cotton mills in Lowell and throughout New England. Through a consolidation of decision-making, the mills helped to increase their profits rather than compete needlessly with each other. The agents of Lowell were also empowered to meet with labor leaders in times of dispute. The Lowell mill agents chose William S. Southworth of the Massachusetts Cotton Mills as their spokesman. He was a prominent member of the community, had served in the state legislature as a Republican, and held membership in several exclusive Lowell clubs. He later became the president of the Lowell Five Cents Savings Bank.

In 1902 the textile operatives of Fall River won a 10% increase in wages. The Lowell Textile Council requested a similar wage hike, but, before a strike threat developed, a local citizens' committee composed of Lowell businessmen concluded that the mills could not afford any increase in wages in 1902, and there was no strike.

In a letter dated February 25, 1903, the Textile Council renewed its demand for a 10% wage increase which would affect some 18,000 operatives in Lowell's seven cotton mills. The letter noted that the Lowell cotton mills had declared dividends during the past year. It also mentioned the unbounded prosperity of the nation as well as Fall River's wage increase. The letter also spoke of a 25% increase in the cost of living since 1899. The Council asked that the increase take effect on Monday, March 30, 1903. There was no threat of a strike, and President Conroy of the Textile Council later announced that there was no talk of a strike in the union circles nor "would a strike need to be resorted to." The labor leaders tried to confine the dispute to the unions and the mill agents, in order to avoid outside influence from any conservative citizens' committee.

The mill agents replied on March 14, 1903, denying the increase for several reasons. The only mills that had profited from the nation's great prosperity, they argued, were those which had modern plants and produced the highest grade of cloth, such as Fall River.

William S. Southworth, Agent of the Massachusetts Mills, c. 1897
(Lowell Museum)

The agents denied that the mills had paid considerable dividends the previous year. The cost of living, they admitted, had gone up, but not 25%. In addition, inflation affected not only the workers, but the mills as well. The mills had to buy large supplies of raw cotton for production at inflated prices. Finally the mill agents claimed that the mills were gradually raising wages as they introduced better goods and machinery, and that their accounts showed materially higher earnings for workers each year.

Upon receiving this refusal, the Lowell Textile Council met and voted to request a conference with the mill agents. The UTW approved this action and assured the Council that the national organization would sustain whatever action the Council took in this matter. Meanwhile the Lowell mills were supported by officials of many New England mills.

A conference between the mill agents and the Council was held on March 19 at the Union National Bank. The agents entered the meeting with a written refusal. The statement, read by Southworth, insisted that the owners took losses before anyone else. Claiming that they were under severe competition from New England and the South, the Lowell mills said they were unable to raise wages by increasing the price of their goods. In order to keep the mills operating, the mills had to offer goods at low prices. Raw materials and supplies had gone up in price since 1902. The mills did not have it in their heart, Southworth went on, to raise wages and then have to reduce them later because of poor market conditions. The statement suggested that Fall River unions would probably urge the Lowell unions to strike, but that Lowell workers should not do so because it would be futile. It stated that union funds could be put to better use, and that, at any event, the strike funds would never equal their wages. Business would be severely hurt, and strikers could only discredit their city and themselves by such an action.

In reply, the Lowell Textile Council simply restated its reasons for the demanded wage increase. The conference failed to head off the strike. The agents had obviously met with the Council only as a formality. They had prepared a written refusal and made no further statements. The Council, on the other hand, had used poor strategy in agreeing to the conference. The Council had prepared cotton goods price lists but did not present them before the meeting adjourned. No ground rules had been set for a true discussion of grievances, and the mill agents came out of the conference well-organized due to Southworth's leadership. The Council appeared weak, since it had not even presented all its arguments at the conference.

Lowell's Board of Trade, which was made up of prominent businessmen, offered to arbitrate, but the Council would have no part of business-dominated arbitration. The Council was determined to strike and requested that the craft unions inaugurate a general strike in Lowell's seven cotton mills. The Council had received no definite financial promises from outside of Lowell; however, it looked to the AFL, the UTW, national loom-fixers, and national mule spinners for support. The skilled operatives, who were not members of their respective craft unions, would be encouraged to join the unions in order to consolidate the strike effort. The Council felt that after a few weeks of idleness, the mills would be forced to run again in order to fulfill their contracts and that there would be an advance in wages.

At the same time as the strike talk proceeded, the UTW president and secretary were trying to arrange another meeting between the mill agents and the Council. In case of failure, an appeal would be made to the State Board of Arbitration. The UTW was obviously following a conservative course before a formal strike vote in order to gain AFL support. However, once the strike was ordered, the national UTW pledged its moral and financial aid. The UTW managed to arrange another conference with the agents. This time two national UTW representatives were present. The request for a wage increase was firmly reiterated and firmly rejected, and the conference ended. The following day the craft unions met and voted to strike.

The Council received several promises of strike aid after the vote. The UTW decided to assess its unions in order to help Lowell, but it was never revealed how much money would be involved. Several local unions in Fall River and New Bedford promised aid, as did Lowell's Trades and Labor Council, representing forty-five non-textile unions in the city. The UTW also recognized the imperative need to organize Lowell's ring spinners in favor of a strike. The ring spinners could undermine the jobs and union of the 280 organized mule spinners. The UTW sent a committee into Lowell to organize the 3,500 female ring spinners, but they were not successful. Further attempts to organize skilled and unskilled operatives would continue into the strike period.

Up to this point in the developing strike, only the skilled union operatives were aware of the situation. The masses of unskilled, low paid, and non-English speaking workers did not have a voice in these decisions. Many did not know about the strike vote or even know the meaning of the word, "strike." It was only after the strike vote that the Council started setting up committees to inform and organize the skilled, non-union workers and some of the unskilled workers. There were still many unskilled workers who were left totally ignorant of the situation for weeks.

In a letter to Agent Southworth, dated March 26, 1903, the Council declared that if an increase was still denied, "we shall cease to work at noon, Saturday, March 28, until such increase asked for is forthcoming." In response, the mill agents announced that the mills would remain open if enough operatives showed up for work.

The business community was deeply concerned by this threatened strike. A strike would cause considerable hardship particularly to small businesses in ethnic neighborhoods. Charles Conant, the President of the Lowell Board of Trade and an important representative of conservative business interests, asked the Textile Council to meet with him in order to avoid a strike. Conroy refused his request. He did not want the conservative interests of small business to defeat labor's struggle. Conant then urged Mayor Charles E. Howe to intervene, but Howe declined. Finally Conant convinced Howe that, under Massachusetts law, the mayor was obliged to notify the State Board of Arbitration of the impending strike. The mayor contacted the State Board, and a date was set for open public hearings in order to consider the situation.

Under Southworth's aggressive leadership, the mill agents transformed the strike into a general lockout. On the morning of March 28, the day that the unions would have struck at noon, notices were posted by the management on the mill gates declaring that the mills would be closed indefinitely. It is doubtful that the mills were shut down because management feared the crippling effects of the strike. It seems more likely that the mills locked the workers out because a shutdown was more profitable at the time: the price of raw cotton had gone up 31% in a few weeks due to a poor harvest. It was more profitable to shut the mills down for several weeks and sell raw cotton; it would also help to break the strike. In addition, some mills had a heavy surplus of finished textile goods on hand and could, therefore, fill orders for some time to come.

They welcomed this opportunity to lock out the operatives, break the strike, and maintain profits.

The Council was greatly damaged by this shutdown because it lost the opportunity to demonstrate its strength. It is, therefore, difficult to determine how much strength the Textile Council actually had. The Lawrence Mill continued to operate even though the mule spinners struck. It was, however, obvious that the unskilled operatives would have worked the day of the shutdown in all the mills. The Greeks, French, Poles, and Portuguese were extremely confused when they came to the closed gates in the morning. For the majority of them, this was the first hint that a wage increase had been requested or a strike threatened. There had obviously been little or no communication between the Textile Council and the unskilled operatives. The Council soon attempted to correct this situation.

The union lists grew rapidly during the first week of the strike. By the end of the week, every mule spinner in the city belonged to the union. Only three out of 175 knappers in the city were not organized. The Textile Council saw this increase as a step in the direction of creating a permanent and strong craft organization in Lowell. The swelling of union lists is better explained, however, by the desire to receive strike aid during a lockout, rather than labor militancy.

The strike, however, prompted the spontaneous organization of unskilled workers along ethnic and job lines. The Greeks, Portuguese, and Poles organized themselves. The Textile Council urged the Greeks to do so, because they seemed to pose the greatest threat to the strike effort. The Greeks made up 4,000 to 5,000 of the mill population, and most were unacquainted with either unions or strikes. Some local Greek labor leaders emerged and claimed to have the support of the whole Greek community, but there was a wide diversity of opinion. Some sympathized with the union efforts because they too would welcome a wage increase. On the other hand, many did not understand why they could not work and earn a day's pay. When the Greek leaders, such as businessman Constantine Anton, announced themselves in favor of the strike, the unions were very pleased. When the Greeks announced that they would even finance their own strike aid and wanted no outside help, the unions were overjoyed. There was no end to the praise that the unions gave the Greeks after they realized that they did not have to pay them any strike funds.

The organization of the Poles and Portuguese was even more rapid. They decided to support the strikers and remain out of work until the wage request was met. The unskilled French-Canadians, who represented a majority of the cotton mill workers in 1903, remained relatively unorganized. Many of the French left to return to Canada or to seek jobs elsewhere in New England. At the end of the first week almost 1,000 had left the city. The Council apparently assumed that the majority of French operatives would leave the city or simply remain passive. The Greeks, Poles, and Portuguese were less mobile, because few had relatives outside of Lowell, and their homelands were too distant for a return trip.

Not only did these ethnic groups organize themselves, but so did the unskilled departments of the mills. They included the ring spinners, spoolers, cloth handlers, firemen, and slasher-tenders. These organizations included some French-Canadians but were predominantly Irish. All these organizations, ethnic and departmental, sent representatives to the Textile Council and were readily welcomed.

The mills, however, had the stronger position at the beginning of the strike and throughout the shut-down, although the Council never admitted it. The price of raw cotton continued to rise, and the mills had a large stock on hand that they could sell. The mills suffered no losses and, at the same time, could undermine the strikers by a lockout.

The Council faced a major defeat during the first week. The Lawrence Mill was still operating after the strike order, even though all the mule spinners had walked out. Ring spinning was used primarily in this mill, and so the mules were dispensable. As a result of UTW encouragement, the Council tried to organize the female ring spinners and knitters in order to stage a walk-out. When the management realized what was happening, it dismissed the labor agitators in the knitting department. Fifteen knitters were fired, and the rest were intimidated. The Council was indignant about this action, but could do nothing. The Council set April 1 as the date for a strike at the Lawrence Mills. On that day, almost all of the 200 knitters and ring spinners showed up for work. The strike order failed badly. The few operatives who had stayed out went back the next day and got their jobs back. The Council had not even attempted to organize the other areas of the Lawrence Mill, and many operatives were still ignorant of the situation. The Council once again used poor strategy against a tough policy by management.

Even with this defeat the Textile Council maintained a confident spirit. The unions still believed that the mills would have to fill cloth orders and, therefore, be obliged to reopen negotiations and increase wages. Unfortunately, the Textile Council never imagined that Greeks, Poles, and Portuguese would be recruited to take over the skilled positions and replace unionists.

During the first week of the strike, the UTW sent a $2,000 check to Lowell. It was to be distributed among local UTW members. The union was also to assess its 200 union affiliates in order to help Lowell. The UTW wanted to give as much strike aid to Lowell as possible because it felt that Lowell was a testing ground for wage increase in the cheaper cotton goods industry. The AFL state organization supported the strike but did not immediately make any financial promises. The national officers of the AFL would also be slow in responding to Lowell's need for strike funds.

The State Board of Arbitration tried to get a settlement in Lowell. Southworth used the hearings to argue the mills' position effectively; the Council failed to present credible counter-arguments. The Board's report supported Southworth and even refused to label the actions of the textile mills a lockout. The "strike" continued.

During the next few weeks the strike began to have its effects on local business. The downtown stores were little affected by the loss of wages in the city. However, by the end of April the loss of $500,000 in operatives' earnings affected the small merchants in the French and Greek neighborhoods. Several grocery stores and other small establishments were forced to close. Tenement owners also found themselves in a precarious situation, because many tenements were vacated by job-seeking operatives. Almost 200 tenements remained empty in Little Canada. For the first time in many years these landlords were forced to advertise for tenants in the newspapers. Many tenements were still inhabited, but the people were not paying rent. Some merchants and landlords agreed to extend credit to the mill operatives because they realized that most of the non-union or unskilled workers had nothing to say about the mills being closed. There were others who extended credit for a short time and then stopped. Some grocers went on a cash-only basis, and some landlords began to evict non-paying tenants. Many businessmen felt sure that the workers would pay their bills once the lockout ended. The small merchants realized that the unskilled workers were forced into unemployment more by the mills' actions than by the strike.

Some of the city's churches began to express their opinion of the strike rather vehemently. In April, the Protestant Ministers' Union of Lowell expressed deep regret at the strike but pleasure at the orderliness that prevailed. By early May the ministers became more critical. Reverend Orville Coats of the Fifth Street Baptist Church said that the strike was ill-advised and that any encouragement to keep the workers out of the mills was a crime. Rev. Coats also declared in a sermon that idleness was a sin and that it was just as sinful for one part of labor to keep another from working. Coats said that he had spoken with Robert Conroy and believed there was no valid reason for the strike. He noted that the strike was causing much suffering, and the masses should have an opportunity to express their opinion of the strike leaders. He ended by shouting, "open the mills, and go to work." Unfortunately, the mills themselves had to agree to reopen before anyone's suffering could end.

The Reverend George E. Martin of the Kirk Street Church, which was attended by many mill agents, enumerated the many kind and charitable acts of the employers. He strongly believed that most labor problems were caused by labor men and not by the capitalists. In the few cases where the owners were to blame, he believed they were answerable directly to God for what they had done. The most vehement opinion was given by Reverend John A. McKnight in the pulpit of the Congregational Church in Dracut. He compared unionism to slavery by saying that the union men were the masters and the non-union men were slaves. He said:

> Don't join anything that will cause debasement to your manhood, whether it be a union or anything else .... Labor gains nothing by strikes, but will by good laws and a better quality and quantity of work.

He went on to discuss the virtues of hard work and individualism. The opinions of these churchmen represented Lowell's wealthy and business-minded Protestant population. The churches of the mill operatives were less public in their views. The Greek church seemed to support, or at least tolerate, the strike in the beginning; its mood, however, changed once the mills reopened. It urged workers back to their jobs. The Irish-Catholic churches backed their unionist congregations throughout the strike. The French-Catholics, like their parishioners, remained neutral and passive.

After two months of idleness, conditions in Lowell greatly worsened. The national craft unions were able to give only subsistence strike benefits to the skilled workers: the mule spinners, loom-fixers, carders, slashers, and weavers. Those skilled workers who joined these unions after the strike order received less strike aid. Those unions that were members of the Textile Council, but not of the national craft unions, used their own local treasuries to support themselves. The unskilled and unorganized operatives of the mills had to apply to the Council to receive what was available out of scarce strike funds. The Lowell Textile Council could not support all the operatives out of work, so it sought contributions. The Council sent circulars throughout the United States and Canada asking various unions for help. The Council also sent delegates to key union areas in the country in order to request funds for the 13,000 Lowell strikers. Delegates were sent to New York City, Chicago, Milwaukee, Philadelphia, Boston, and many other cities. The UTW was also helpful in requesting aid. The Council did receive some contributions but not enough to support about 13,000 people for eight weeks.

The Lowell Textile Council felt obliged to try to take care of locked out operatives. The Overseers of the Poor would not meet the needs of people on strike. The State Board of Charity told the Textile Council that it could only give aid to the strikers when all the funds were completely exhausted. The Council had set up an investigation committee of fourteen members to grant aid to operatives; in May, however, the committee was abolished by Conroy for corruption. The committee had given money to people who were never employed in the textile mills. The Executive Committee of the Council took over the investigating from then on.

There were numerous reports of destitution, near-starvation, evictions, and even a suicide due to the strike. One woman was evicted from her tenement with her three children. She got fifty cents one week from the Council, and a dollar another week, and that was all. One woman had no savings, no friends, and no family in Lowell. She was evicted from her boarding house and spent the night wandering about the city until she was found the next day. In desperation, she had taken poison and died.

Few Greeks, Portuguese or Poles ever applied for strike aid. The *Boston Transcript* and the *Courier-Citizen* both studied the conditions of operatives in Lowell and reported that many operatives had savings that they could draw upon. In many families one or more members were employed outside of the cotton mills, so there was at least some money available. But the sad state of the operatives was also apparent. There were Greek, French, and Polish operatives who were near starvation and who did not know where or how to get aid. Some had favored the strike, but after two months of deprivation, many operatives deeply desired to return to work because their situation made it an absolute necessity.

Conroy firmly denied that any destitution existed because of the strike. He said that there was no more than the usual suffering in Lowell and that his committee was attending to every deserving case. It was apparent that many people were too proud to admit their condition. The Greeks, for example, preferred to deplete their savings. On the other hand, the Textile Council could not accept the argument that suffering existed because of the strike. Perhaps it if had admitted that a lockout existed, it could have denounced the destitution that was prevalent. As it was, the Council had to believe that it had an efficient aid-distribution committee headed by Conroy, and it could win the strike.

After two months the mill agents revealed their plans. Jobs would be available when enough people wished to return to work. In so many words the mills said they would end the lockout, when the Council ended the strike. The mills had waited just long enough to make this offer. The unorganized workers were almost starved into submission, and the unionists were also facing hard times after two months of idleness.

At the end of May, AFL President Samuel Gompers came to Lowell to speak with the unionists. The union leaders had asked him to come to Lowell at the beginning of the strike. At that time Conroy felt that Gompers would not only stimulate hope but would also bring national recognition and, therefore, more sympathy and money to the strikers. Gompers had been on a major speaking tour during most of April, so he delayed his visit until he came to the New England area for other commitments. Unfortunately, Gompers' arrival did not bring the desired results.

Gompers disappointed a crowd of 4,000 people in Lowell on May 25, 1903. He expounded the advantages of trade unionism, justified the strike in Lowell, and then went on to say that the AFL would help the Lowell workers but would not assess funds from its membership. The AFL was to issue circulars to be sent to all organized labor in the United States requesting aid. Of course, this had already been done by the Textile Council two months before. Gompers did not express enthusiasm for the Lowell strike, when he stated:

> I do not think that so much money will come to Lowell as came to the [coal] miners, but I hope that it will come in sufficient amounts to enable you to buy bread and maintain your manhood and woman-hood; and if you fail, it will not be my fault.

Gompers did not say why he would not assess AFL members in order to help Lowell, yet it was fairly clear that he believed the situation in Lowell to be futile. By offering only voluntary aid, he failed to restore morale and seemed to indicate that the Textile Council should call off a hopeless strike.

Gompers' visit undermined the unionists. The newspapers were quick to note that even the great labor leader did not whole-heartedly support the Lowell strike. With this last blow to the strikers' morale, the mill agents decided to reopen the mills. The mills had waited long enough to insure the fact that most non-unionists would return to work out of sheer desperation and that dissension would weaken the union ranks. On May 27 the knappers' union lost seventeen members. These men had joined the union after the strike order was given. They went to work in the Tremont and Suffolk Mills in order to prepare the machines for the opening of the mills.

On May 26 the mill agents sent a notice to the newspapers. The mills would open their gates on June 1, and all workers would be allowed to return. The old wages were in effect, and there would be no discrimination against strikers. The mills stated that they could have kept the mills closed longer and still sold their raw cotton for a profit of up to $10 a bale. However, the mills said they would not treat the workers in this fashion. The agents believed that the operatives would return happily. If the operatives did their work satisfactorily, they would not be discharged. All the operatives were given one week to return to work. This time period would give the workers who had left Lowell the opportunity to return. At the week's end, the mills would hire outside help, if they did not have enough operatives. By putting this one-week clause into the notice, the mill agents intended to break the unions' strength. If a union striker stayed out of work after June 8, he probably would never work again in a Lowell mill. The choice was between work or the union.

The reaction to the reopening notice was very enthusiastic. The French-Canadians, Greeks, Poles, and Portuguese were, on the whole, very eager to return to work. Constantine Anton, the Greek labor leader, at first said that the Greeks would not return to work until all the unions decided to do so. Anton was quick, however, to change his opinion after speaking with his fellow Greeks. The next day he claimed that he had been misquoted and said that he "did not know" whether they would return to work. Greek merchants also believed that the Greeks would return to work, because they had extended all the credit that they possibly could. The French community was overjoyed by the chance to return to work, and families were busy notifying friends who had left the city. The small business community was very pleased by the reopening of the mills. The landlords and grocers who had extended credit for the nine weeks of the strike announced that they would give no further credit to the operatives after June 1 unless payments on the bills began.

The Textile Council firmly stated that the reopening of the mills would be a failure because the skilled operatives would not go back. Conroy claimed that many of the unions had increased membership and that many skilled operatives had left the city and would be difficult to replace. He said that no union man who was truly honorable would return to work and claimed he represented 7,000 organized textile workers. He said that unofficial picket lines would be used when the mills reopened in order to keep labor away from the gates. Conroy promised that only moral suasion would be used to convince the workers to remain on strike. The Council asked for another conference with the mill agents, but the agents flatly refused. The mills knew that they had won.

The unions even resorted to increasing their strike benefits for their members in order to quash any dissent. The mule spinners went so far as to give the ring spinners part of their union strike aid to keep them out. The mule spinners had received reports that the mills were increasing the numbers of ring spinners and getting rid of the remainder of their mules. They realized that the ring spinners could undermine their whole craft, so the mule spinners were desperate to keep them away from the mill gates.

The gates of the mills finally opened on June 1, and as they did, the unions of the Textile Council held meetings. Holding the meetings while the gates were reopening gave the union strikers an ultimatum: his union or his job. If a member did not show up for his union's meeting, then it was assumed he had gone back to work, and he was blacklisted by the union. If a member went to the union meeting, he still had to contemplate whether or not he might lose his job after a week.

Of all the craft unions, the mule spinners were still the best organized. However, in all the other unions, there were varying degrees of desertion. Not only did some union men appear for work on June 1, but many hundreds of unskilled workers did also. It was reported that throngs of Greeks, Poles, Portuguese and French-Canadians were seen on their way to work very early in the morning. When the gates finally opened, management announced that there were enough operatives to run the mills. The mills gave out the percentages of the full force of operatives at work on June 1:

Massachusetts Mill	33%
Merrimack	60%
Boott	45%
Hamilton	65%
Appleton	65%
Tremont	40%

Both sides claimed a victory that day. The mill agents said that they were able to run the mills successfully, while the Textile Council claimed that the mills could not run for long without the 2,000 union members who were still on strike.

The next few days saw an increase in the work force at the mills and a further blacklisting by the unions of disloyal members. For the most part, the union men, who had originally voted for a strike nine weeks earlier, remained loyal to their cause. Those who had joined the unions after the strike started began to desert. The picket lines that were set up at the mills were unable to prevent the return to work. Some of the unskilled, immigrant women were, at first, hesitant to pass the picket lines, but when they realized that no harm would come to them, they entered the mills.

As the Textile Council remained out on strike, the mills were undergoing an unusual shift in the labor force. The labor leaders did not fully realize the great advantage the situation gave to the Portuguese, Poles, and Greeks. Eager for advancement and ambitious to learn, these people were trained and moved into the skilled jobs of the unionists on strike. Many of these people had supported the strike for nine weeks, but during that time they received no strike

aid from the Council. Sheer necessity forced them to return to the
mills. The mills promised them that they would retain their new
positions, even if the union men eventually returned. In this way,
the mills not only gained a loyal and cheaper labor force but also
succeeded in undermining the unionism that had prevailed in the
skilled departments.

For three weeks the mills ran well without the craft unionists,
and cloth was being shipped out of the city. The Textile Council,
with all fourteen unions represented, finally voted to call off the
strike. Thereupon the mill agents announced that the mills would
not be running at full capacity after all because of competitive
market conditions. Therefore, not all strikers who returned to work
could possibly be re-employed. The mills intended to refuse work
to unionists and destroy the Council. Many skilled positions had already been filled, either by Lowell operatives or outside help, and
not all of the strikers got their old jobs back. A handful of mule
spinners were rehired, but the majority were not. Several members
of the Textile Council Executive Board did not get their jobs back,
notably President Conroy. Agent Southworth said that Conroy
would not be hired at the Massachusetts because he had left work
on February 21, before the strike began. Therefore, Conroy was
listed as quitting, and he had no right to receive his job back because he was not officially a striker. Conroy had been blacklisted.

The 1903 Lowell strike was a failure for several reasons. The Textile Council had chosen an inappropriate time to strike. The price
of raw cotton was very high because of a poor harvest in 1902, and,
therefore, producing cloth was unprofitable. Agent Southworth
finally admitted in June that if it hadn't been for the strike, the
mills would have shut down anyway because of the high price of
raw cotton. The mills were able to close and still make a profit by
selling off their supplies of raw cotton. The mills obviously did not
shut down because they feared a devastating strike; they locked out
the operatives.

In addition to this poor timing, the UTW and AFL did not give
sufficient support to the morale or financial needs of the strikers.
The UTW was still a weak national organization and did not command the support of its local unions. As a result, the UTW could
not raise money without difficulty, because the strong local autonomy of the craft unions had not yet been overcome. The AFL national did not give full support to the Lowell strike because it foresaw
its eventual defeat. From the beginning of the strike, the mills had

the unions on the defensive, and Gompers quickly concluded that the strike was futile.

The ultimate failure of the strike resulted from the craft union mentality. These exclusive craft unions did not feel any responsibility to the unorganized and the unskilled. The Council's strategy and decisions were fundamentally concerned with the interests of skilled Irish workers. It was difficult for all workers to feel union solidarity when their cultural backgrounds, nationalities, and job categories were unrepresented. The Lowell Textile Council, by its very make-up, indicated that it catered to the skilled and better-paid members of the textile mills, predominantly Irish-Americans and some French-Canadians. It was only after the strike was ordered that the Council made an effort to inform and rally the support of the unskilled labor. Its efforts were unsuccessful because the Council did not communicate with or represent all the workers. When the mills reopened, the unskilled saw their opportunity to advance and took it. They had not been educated by the unions, nor did they feel any real kinship with the unionists.

The results of this unsuccessful strike were important to Lowell's textile industry. Wages remained at the 1902 levels. The rest of the New England textile industry was relieved. The Lowell mills had duped the community into believing a strike actually existed and received no rebuke for the lockout from most of Lowell's business community, clergy, the State Board of Arbitration, nor even the Lowell Textile Council. By the end of the strike the Lowell mills had maintained their very strong anti-union position. The manufacturers were building up a new ethnic labor force of skilled operatives — non-union men and women — who might remain loyal to the mills. These newly promoted workers undermined the unions' positions in the Lowell mills by taking over skilled jobs. This new labor force seemed less likely to organize and strike. Many unionists did not find jobs in Lowell after the strike and had to move out of the city or into different industries. The union leadership especially suffered. The strongest union in Lowell, the mule spinners, was totally undermined by unskilled ring spinners. The UTW had lost much strength in Lowell because its union men were replaced, and its treasury was depleted.

In reality the strike indicated that the craft unions could simply not attempt to stop mill production without the cooperation of all mill operatives. The mill managers were united and strong enough to undermine the craft unions by using cheap new immigrant labor or new machines in their place. The mills could maintain this advantage because of Southworth's aggressive leadership and the cotton industry's cooperation in New England. In order to command the respect of mill management, craft unions would have to give way to industrial unions which were concerned with the improvement of all mill labor rather than just a part of it. It was obvious by June of 1903 that craft unionism had proven to be an anachronism in the Lowell cotton mills.

GREEK WORKERS IN THE MILLS OF LOWELL

Lewis T. Karabatsos and Dale Nyder

The Greeks in Lowell were like many other ethnic groups in the city. Economic and political upheavals in their native country had forced them to emigrate to the United States with the hope of doing better for themselves and their families. Once here, the Greeks also experienced the hardships which accompany those who enter a new culture with different customs and traditions, but they quickly became an important force within the city's working community.

The first Greek settler in Lowell was a peddler who in 1880 was referred to simply as Depontis. Little is known of this fruit vendor, who took the American name of Peter. Those who followed him probably found their way to Lowell from the established Greek communities in New Orleans, New York, and Chicago. By 1884 chocolates and Turkish candy were available from a Greek who had his stand in the alley alongside the old City Hall on Merrimack Street. These few men began the Greek community in the city.

Soon members of their small group sought employment in the textile mills. They were put to work at unskilled jobs in the picker and dye rooms at wages of about four dollars a week. In early 1894 approximately 130 Greeks were employed at the Lawrence Corporation and a few more in the Tremont and Suffolk Mills. The typical Greek immigrant to Lowell in the 1890s was a male between eighteen and twenty-five years old. In 1896 one woman and her two daughters were the only Greek females in the community.

Costas Liacopolous, in an interview in 1973, remembered his ex-periences as a young man traveling by ship to the United States at the turn of the century. He described his accommodations as having "one floor, all kinds of beds, all sleep together . . . not clean, lots of bugs." One can imagine the disillusionment he felt coming from the fresh air, sunshine, and open space of the Greek country-side. All his negative feelings were, however, momentarily dis-pelled when, in his own words:

> . . . I come to Staten Island [New York]. When I come out, I found a dime on the street. Jesus, I said, Christ's sake, I just come here, I begin to get rich now!

Like Liacopolous, many dreamed of riches, but few found them easily. Once in Lowell, most Greeks were taken in by friends or relatives who would also try to find employment for them in the mills. A few started their own businesses within the community, but almost all Greeks worked as unskilled laborers in the textile factories. Management began to appreciate their steady work habits and recruited them actively. This recruitment of the Greek worker created tension between the Hellenic community and the Irish and French-Canadian groups, longer established as workers in the mills.

Exploitation of the Greek mill worker took many forms. An over-seer might hire a new recruit and not pay him for a while, calling it a learning period. The young Greek would continue working for no money until his fellow-workers noticed his situation. The wil-lingness of Greeks to work for low wages to keep their jobs, coupled with their desire to save money to send home or to bring over family members, also served to further antagonize the Irish and French-Canadian workers. Overseers used this to their advan-tage by threatening to replace recalcitrants with incoming Greek workers. These threats provided the basis for ethnic hostility within the mills.

The mill managers also tried to use the Greeks as strikebreakers. In 1900 the dyers at the Hamilton went out on strike, but the hun-dred Greeks who were hired to take their places were persuaded by the strikers not to work. However, in September of the same year, 400 print workers at the Merrimack refused to work overtime unless they were paid time-and-a-quarter. When their jobs were filled by Greeks, the strike spread to 200 employees in the packing department. Armed guards were assigned to the Greeks to escort them to and from the mill. When the strike ended on October 5, the Greeks remained in their positions while only 115 of the 600 striking workers were taken back. Cooperation with mill management, which led to hostility from other ethnic groups, was dangerous to the Greek community in Lowell. They quickly learned to operate independently of both the mill owners and organized labor unions dominated by the Irish.

Jobs and wage disputes were not the only concern of the early Greek community. Because of obvious language and culture differences, the early Greek residents feared that their religious and cultural heritage might be lost in the United States. To avoid this, they established a society known as the Washington-Acropolis to perpetuate their Greek Orthodox faith and traditions. Its membership of 150 men included not only textile workers, but also the peddlers who were to become the future store owners and businessmen of the community. On August 24, 1895, the *Lowell Morning Citizen* announced that a branch of the Greek Church had been organized and a permanent priest obtained. The newspaper credited the community with 450 inhabitants, most of whom were represented in the congregation of the Washington-Acropolis. The organization's meetings and religious services were held in public halls while they raised money for a building of their own.

The early male immigrants to Lowell crowded together in small apartments. In this way, they were able to live together and save money by sharing expenses and household duties. At times, those with jobs supported others who were unemployed. Wages were so meager that renting anything other than the dilapidated buildings in the once-Irish neighborhood, the Acre, was out of the question. Regardless of poor living conditions, however, the community began to develop. After the formation of the Washington-Acropolis and the integration of Greeks into the industrial work force, the Greek Acre began to grow. A coffeehouse, essential to male social life, opened, followed by stores for Greek food and supplies and more coffeehouses.

The religious needs grew quickly with additional population, and on February 11, 1900, there were enough Greeks to organize the Greek Orthodox Community of the Holy Trinity. Once established in Lowell, it worked with the Greek community in New York to obtain religious furnishings for its services. In February 1901 the community purchased an apartment house on the corner

of Lewis and Jefferson Streets from Patrick Keys for $6,500 in antic-
ipation of building a church. Of that amount, $1,050 was raised by
the community, and the balance was borrowed from the Lowell
Five Cent Savings Bank. An adjacent building was purchased for
$2,800 in 1903 and financed by the same bank.

While the community saved and planned for the church which
was to be the center of its religious and cultural life, the immediate
problems of living in poor, over-crowded housing and working in
the cotton mills created a medical crisis. Tuberculosis appeared
among the Greeks around 1900 and continued to spread during
subsequent years. The disease threatened to become epidemic, but
by 1905 attempts were made to control it. A number of younger
physicians in the city began a tuberculosis campaign among the
Greeks in the Acre. They held an exhibition in Matthew Hall on
Dutton Street, which reminded the community of their healthy
lives in the homeland and their need for fresh air and sunshine.
The Middlesex Women's Club also published a pamphlet on the
prevention of tuberculosis. The pamphlet was effective, partly because it had been translated into Greek. One Greek coffeehouse
owner on Market Street was so concerned about the problem that
he had large shower baths installed in his building so that men
whose apartments contained no bathing facilities could take show-
ers. Women were allowed to use them at special hours. Neither the
local doctors, the philanthropic club women, nor the Greek community linked diseased lungs to the cotton lint breathed in by most
mill workers.

By 1905 a number of Greek women had made their way to
Lowell. These included young, single women who were "matched"
and married to the many eligible bachelors of the colony. Marriage
and family life improved the living conditions among the Greeks
and also forestalled the threat of inter-marriage with other ethnic
groups. The community changed rapidly as a result, and the focus
of its activities shifted away from the young, single male to the
more stable family unit. These marriages of young Greek men and
women assured the survival of Greek culture and religion in
Lowell through their children. The development of family units
also meant that more living space was needed as well as higher
wages.

After the strike of 1903 the Greek community became involved
in its own independent acts of labor militancy. In 1905 fifty-five
Greek spinners working in the Merrimack Mill struck because of a

dispute involving a change in overseers, but they returned to work two days later without resolution of their grievance. In December of the same year, eighty Greek spinners and twisters in the Merrimack struck once again against an alleged wage cut. They returned to work one week later when the dispute was settled amicably. Forty-three Greek spinners at the Tremont and Suffolk left work in August 1906, demanding an increase in wages. The following month sixty-five Greek workers in the Lowell Machine Shop struck against an objectionable overseer. When the overseer was replaced, the strikers returned to work.

Many times the Greek strikers would return to work without a resolution of their demands to change working conditions. For many, the community's need for steady work and economic security far outweighed the potential of collective action in a strike. According to Liacopolous:

Greeks save money so they'll be better. We work hard and we save money. We work hard for our own security. I sacrificed a lot of things to put money aside for a rainy day . . . .

Liacopolous' views may shed light on the attitudes of the early Greek community, especially toward unions dominated by other ethnic groups:

I didn't like the idea of labor unions. Unions go overboard. I want them to compromise, not to strike. Unions never give us anything. Anything I got, I got myself. They don't give anything . . . .

Another early Greek immigrant, Spiros Los, supported the Liacopoulas statement:

I always against them [the unions]. Not capable of job if you strike. A good man can get job anywhere . . . . The little you get, you get every week. Strikes always started by a wise guy. If you don't like job, get another one.

When the Greek mill workers did go out on strike, they invariably chose a businessman of their community as their spokesman to deal with management. In a strike situation, they were Greeks first, and workers second.

Constantine Anton, the owner of a Greek fruit store, was well-known for his involvement as a representative of Greek workers in the strikes of 1903, 1905, and 1906. In April 1907 he again

Constantine Anton, second from left, July, 1917
(Lowell Museum/Anton Collection.)

represented his community during a walkout from the Bigelow
Carpet Company over a wage dispute. The Carpet Company, located on lower Market Street, abutted the Greek Acre and employed
Greeks in the dye house, the mill yards and the various sections of
the wool department. These jobs, among the least desirable in the
mills, involved not only great physical labor, as in the case of the
yard hands who loaded and unloaded materials, but also a good
deal of danger, including the unhealthy conditions that the wool
scourers and dyers were exposed to.

The strike began on April 3, when fifty employees of the dye
house, reportedly Greeks, Armenians and Turks, walked out
demanding a 10% wage increase. The following day the strikers
and their sympathizers gathered outside the mill gate, causing a
minor disturbance which led to the arrest of one striker. Later that
afternoon, the strikers returned and, according to the *Lowell Courier
Citizen*:

... more than 1,000 people swarmed lower Market Street with the ex-
pectation that the situation would result in a small sized riot.

The presence of police supposedly halted the riot, and the crowd
dispersed. That evening Bigelow Agent William K. Fairbanks
issued a statement to the effect that he did not know the reasons for
the strike but assumed it to be a dispute about wages. And, if it
were, the Greeks had made "no formal application" to the company
concerning an increase. He also dismissed the entire situation by
pointing out that the activity was "a sort of spring feeling they [the
Greeks] get." Fairbanks' statement to the press was contradicted in
the succeeding days of the strike. His reference to the motivation of
the Greeks as a "spring feeling" indicated that the policy of the
Bigelow Company would be to discredit the Greek workers as a nationality, insult and divide them, and hope to make them give up
their demands and return to work.

On April 8 the *Lowell Sun* published an editorial initially in support of the strike. Although the newspaper felt that "it is none of
our business," the editor did believe that "it is bad policy to treat
strikers, however weak in numbers, with utter defiance." If the
Bigelow management was "gouging" its employees by not paying
fair wages, then the best thing to do would be to comply with the
wage increase demanded and allow everyone to get back to work.
On the same day, Constantine Anton defended the position of the
strikers and offered a different version of Fairbanks' statement concerning the wage request. The strikers, according to Anton, never
had an opportunity to speak with Fairbanks because when their
demands were brought to the attention of the overseer, "he told
them they could go; that they need not look for any increase in
wages."

The *Courier-Citizen* on April 9 reported that all the Greeks
wanted a 10% increase but thought that the strikers would be replaced. Although the *Citizen* did not believe that Fairbanks would
grant any wage increase, it reported that he had assured State Arbitration Board member, Charles Palmer, that there would be no discrimination made against the strikers if they returned to work. The
Bigelow agent went on to say that it was impossible to raise wages
under the present conditions of the company. One month later,
however, Fairbanks would announce quite a different policy.

Lowell's other newspaper, the *Sun,* carried a front-page story on
the same day as the *Citizen* article, which attacked the reputation of

the Greek community and also used scandal to undermine the
unity of the strike. The headlines read that Michael Iatros, one of
the pillars of local Lowell Greek society, had been arrested and
charged with conspiracy to defraud the federal government in an
immigration case. Iatros was a Greek immigrant who had come to
Lowell in 1893, when he was employed as a common mill hand at
the Lawrence Manufacturing Company. He gained a reputation
during the Greco-Turkish War when, from Lowell, he expounded
his "declaration of patriotism" for his native land and returned to
Greece. Being too late to fight in the war, however, he came back to
Lowell where he advanced himself within the best social circles of
the city and eventually married an "American" woman. Because of
his fluency in six languages, Iatros became the Greek consul for the
Hellenic community in Lowell and served as a federal interpreter
in Boston.

The federal charges against Iatros stemmed from an incident in
1904 when he, as an interpreter, allegedly allowed two young
Greeks, who were ineligible to enter the United States, to pass
through Immigration on the basis that they had parents in Lowell
who would vouch for them. Iatros, it was alleged, took the two
boys to New York where he was able to secure jobs for them. The
boys, as it later turned out, were not the sons of Greek residents,
but only nephews. The newspapers had begun to focus more heavily on the Iatros story than the events surrounding the Greeks on
strike.

The *Sun* printed a letter on April 10 which momentarily shifted
the news back to the strike issues. Not only did the letter thank the
paper for its editorial support on April 8, but it made quite clear the
Greek position on labor militancy. The Greeks had been insulted,
their honor and pride had been threatened:

Lowell, Massachusetts
April 9, 1907

Mr. Editor: We, the strikers of the Bigelow Carpet Co., at a meeting
held last night voted to remain out until our request for a ten per cent
increase has been granted and we have appointed Mr. Constantine P.
Anton our representative.

He will take the matter up at any time with Mr. Fairbanks and we
will stand by whatever agreement may be reached.

We feel sorry and surprised that Mr. Fairbanks, the agent of the
carpet mills, should have given the police orders to arrest us when

we were not making any trouble. Of course it is easy for men who earn $6.80 a week to pay fines of $25, $15 and $10. It is easy on such big wages to support a family and pay fines in police court.

We do not believe in strikes and it is not our fault that we are out on strike. We realize that it is best to settle all differences in an amicable way and that was what we tried to do and we made our request in a respectful way to the overseer.

He got mad in a minute and said he would not listen to our request, that we were getting all we were worth and if we didn't like it, to get out.

We think it was wrong for the overseer to use us in that way. If he had used us kindly and asked us to wait until such time as he could take the matter up with the agent, we would have waited and for that reason we think we are not to blame.

We are strangers in this country and we came here to work. We do not like to be out on strike, but we will not work for $6.80 a week.

The opinion expressed editorially in the Lowell Sun on Monday evening was the best that we have seen, and we wish to thank The Sun for such expression. We also wish to thank Hon. Charles D. Palmer for his kindness towards us and interest in us.

Fair-Minded Striker

Two other incidents were reported on the same day. The first was a disclaimer from the Appleton Company that all its Greek employees were being discharged. The *Lowell Sun* reporter investigating the story not only interviewed an Appleton official, who considered the rumor unfounded, but also visited the Market Street coffeehouses and found them empty, indicating the Greeks were, in fact, working. Inquiries into the possible firing of Greeks in other mills corroborated the reporter's findings. When asked about his role in this and previous strikes, Constantine Anton answered that "I . . . advised my people . . . to bring about a settlement of difficulties before going out on strike." He further stated that he would have preferred the Greeks to approach the agent about their concerns but, having approached the overseer first, they were told "to get out, that they were no good." Greek honor and pride had been insulted. As their leader, Anton wanted peaceful negotiations between labor and management but, when they were treated with disrespect, he backed the workers' strike action with the statement: "I stand for justice as well as [industrial] peace."

The *Courier-Citizen*, on the other hand, printed nothing on behalf of the strikers but carried in bold headlines Iatros' plea of not guilty to the federal authorities. The charges included falsifying information to the Immigration Department and also charging a fee of $15 per person to incoming immigrants for his services. The investigation and subsequent arrest of Iatros was the result of a complaint submitted to the State Department by Lowell's Reverend Panos Ginieres, who accused the Consul of "accepting money from Greek immigrants on his assurance that he could insure their being landed." Iatros stated that he was glad that the matter had been brought to a head, because he had been annoyed at the allegations and the months of investigation. He said that he was ready to face the charges in open court and was certain that he could meet them without difficulty.

On April 11 a new Greek Consul was named to replace Michael Iatros. Market Street grocer, George Conzoules, was temporarily appointed to the post by the Consul General in New York. Conzoules was the choice of Iatros, and the designation of the temporary consul was immediately approved from Greece through the New York office.

While Iatros waited for a grand jury hearing, a conference was held on April 11 between Fairbanks and Anton with Charles Palmer sitting in as the state arbitrator. Fairbanks demanded that the workers return to work that day under the existing scale of wages. If they did not, the company would not even consider investigating the possibility of a wage increase. The Greeks refused to accept these terms and declared that they would continue to stay out until the increase was granted.

Strikebreakers, brought in from Nashua, New Hampshire, were dissuaded from working by the strikers, who also vowed that "no Greeks will take the places of the men now out." Anton, interviewed for his reaction to the request, stated that the Greeks would have cooperated with management by not striking had they "been treated like human beings instead of animals . . . ." He supported the Greeks' right as workers to express their concerns to management and repeated that when they were told by the overseer to get out, they had no choice but to strike. Anton defended the strikers' militancy and emphasized that $6.80 was not "a fair wage compared with the wages paid for similar work in other mills." He also described the dye house atmosphere as "a cloud of vapor so dense that they cannot see five feet in front of them." He reminded the public of "the Greek who was killed in a vat in the dye house not long ago."

The Greeks were emphasizing through Anton their decision not to return to work without an increase. If they returned without a change in wages, they believed that they would eventually have to strike again. Anton stated that the Bigelow Carpet Company could not get anyone else "for the work these men did for less than $8.00 a week." Americans wouldn't do it, and he reminded management that the strikers had proven that even Greek strikebreakers would not take these places.

On April 12 the Bigelow management took a strong stand against the Greeks as a national group. Declaring that the mill would "get along without them," it went on to try to discredit the group by calling them "unskilled" and "altogether too ready to stand together when a question of wages showed itself." Furthermore, the company offered the wage of $8.00 per week ($1.20 more than the Greeks were making) to anyone — other than a Greek — who wanted to work in the mill. This higher figure was based on the demand of the strikers who had wanted $9.00 per week (an increase of $2.20), but had stated that they would settle for $8.00. As a result, the company humiliated the Greeks by offering their desired increase to any other nationality. The strikers were also blacklisted.

Despite the company's public indifference to the effect of the strike on the production, it was reported that forty-seven cars loaded with coal and various supplies had been left in the yard and that management had been unable to get anyone to unload them. Bigelow's plant in Clinton, which normally got two carloads of yarn per week from Lowell, did not receive any during the first week of the strike. The wool departments were also affected in the scouring, spinning, carding, doubling, reeling, and combing departments. The company, therefore, sent eight employees out on a hiring mission but could not find anyone to take the place of the Greeks in the dye houses. They did, however, have some luck in hiring twenty men to fill the vacant positions in the wool department at wages of $8.50 a week. Six Lithuanians were eventually found to work in the dye house, but, when word got around to the Greeks, they followed the men to their homes in Bent's Court and convinced them not to return to work the next day. The labor recruiters for Bigelow were under pressure. They were told to fill the positions with only English-speaking men and found the demand unusual and unprecedented. One stated that to his knowledge, "such a thing was never done before in this city." The recruiters, despite their canvassing in saloons and on the streets, met with little success. Many would not work to replace the strikers for fear of being called strikebreakers, while others, it was reported, told the recruiter, "that a Greek was just as good as any other man . . .," and they would not, therefore, take their positions. The recruiters did eventually manage to find ten idle men to work in the dye houses.

The strikers, through Anton, defended themselves again in a letter to the *Courier-Citizen*, dated April 12. He argued that the Greeks were being singled out as the only ones involved in the strike, when in actuality other nationalities — Armenians and Turks — were involved. Other departments in the mill, firemen and carpenters, were asking for increases and, therefore, it was not just the Greeks doing so. The Greek community, stung by attacks from the press and management, was reaching out to other ethnic groups and workers in different jobs. The vulnerability of striking as a single nationality was becoming clear to the Greeks.

All seemed to be quiet for the next few days until, once again, large front-page headlines focussed on the Iatros case. A *Sun* story April 17 reported that Iatros faced the grand jury, which charged him with only one count, not three as originally reported, of conspiracy against the United States government. His bail, which was easily raised, was set at $1,000. The *Sun* also ran a large cartoon of young Greek boys working in the mill. Beneath it, a story reported that the immigration authorities were investigating an alleged conspiracy to bring Greek boys into the country illegally. Terming it a "padrone" system, which were labor contracts notoriously exploitative of immigrant labor, the report in the *Sun* focussed on the problem solely within the Greek community. Although admitting that "the alleged conspiracy is not confined to Greeks alone . . .," it skimmed over the involvement of other nationalities.

The *Sun* on April 27 reported a "very persistent rumor" that Bigelow, on May 1, would announce a 10% increase in wages. Although Bigelow would not confirm the rumor, it was assumed that the increase would come and the strike was "practically over." A mill official did state, however, that while dye house help was short, "there are so many nationalities represented that it is not likely that any one will organize trouble." This was an indication that the company would never again be dependent on one single ethnic group to occupy the majority of positions in a particular section or department.

Without much fanfare, the May 1 issue of the *Lowell Sun* simply announced that Michael Iatros had been acquitted of all charges against him. There was no explanation given for the verdict of the U.S. District Court in Boston. Furthermore, over the next few days, the newspapers created an atmosphere which proved highly prejudicial to the community. Ridiculous stories began to appear stressing the violent and irrational nature of the Greeks. Articles about murders among their numbers and a series on "An Insane Greek" who ended up in the City Farm because of "unreciprocated love" seemed only to justify Bigelow's actions to ban all Greeks from their payroll.

Finally, on May 7, the *Sun* reported that a 5% wage increase had gone into effect the day before for about 1,000 employees at the Bigelow. Fairbanks, in an interview in the *Courier-Citizen* on the same day, stated that the increase was "a case of re-apportioning the money . . . . In some departments, the men were underpaid, and the wages unequally distributed." Fairbanks admitted that the decision was made "a few days ago" and that no official notices were posted. Piece workers were not eligible for the increase because "as a rule, they were well paid . . .," and the yard hands, who were part of the strike movement, had been working on a new wage schedule for sometime. Fairbanks assured the press that the yard hand situation had been settled earlier and "none of those Greeks who went out are working now . . . ." The Bigelow Company was concentrating on hiring non-Greeks but in order to do so had to increase wages.

The strike was over. The Bigelow Carpet Company had done everything in its power to discredit the Greek community. While the company was being pressured to give in to the workers' demands, the arrest of Michael Iatros conveniently overshadowed the Greek plight in the mills. As more and more stories about the Greeks appeared in the papers, Fairbanks found it easier to justify his blacklisting of striking workers. Once that was accomplished, the Greeks had lost. When Michael Iatros was acquitted of his charges, Bigelow quietly gave a small wage increase to its employees and eliminated all Greeks. Many sought and received positions in other mills, while others, not able to withstand the month-long strike, had moved to other cities looking for work.

In June 1910 Anton was again called upon by the Greeks to help settle a strike of 200 spinners and doffers at the Massachusetts and Prescott Mills. Based on a demand for a 10% wage increase for both jobs, the strike lasted approximately two weeks and included a fund-raising event during which the community collected $1200. However, after meeting with management's strategist of the 1903 strike, William S. Southworth, agent of the Massachusetts Mills, Anton, apparently influenced by Southworth, persuaded the Greek workers to abandon half of their strike demands and to press only for a wage increase for the doffers. Two-thirds of the Greek strikers followed Anton's leadership and returned to work; the rest were displaced.

As families grew in size, the demands placed on the community increased. Businesses catering to the needs of Greeks developed along Market and Dummer Streets. In 1906 the community, having experienced strikes, health problems and culture-shock, was, nonetheless, able to lay the cornerstone of its church. The buildings bought in 1901 and 1903 were razed, and on October 29, 1906, the *Lowell Sun* carried this description of the event:

> ... with ceremonies imposing and impressive, the corner stone of the new Greek Church at the corner of Jefferson and Lewis Streets was laid .... About 1,000 Greeks marched from Matthew's Hall on Dutton Street through Market Street to the site of the new Church, headed by St. Patrick's Cadet Band. ...

> A copper box containing papers was placed in the cornerstone. On the papers was [sic] inscribed the names of President Roosevelt and King George of Greece and the Metropolitan of Athens, Theolitos.

The money to build the church had been raised through collections from the community. The parishioners contributed some or all of their weekly salaries and gold jewelry as well. Their pride and enthusiasm seemed to dispel, momentarily, any ethnic rivalry for, as the *Sun* account relates, the music used for the laying of the cornerstone was provided by St. Patrick's Catholic Church, located across the canal on Suffolk Street.

The Greek Orthodox Church of Holy Trinity was finally opened in March 1908 with the performance of the first Liturgy. The structure not only represented the first Greek Orthodox Church to be built in New England, but also the first Byzantine-styled structure to be built in the United States, specifically to house Greek Orthodox worship. Based on the Agia Sophia in Istanbul, the Holy Trinity represented an important focus for the city's growing Greek population.

The church provided an impressive religious institution which also became a center for community events. During strikes in 1910 and 1912, the church was the site for organizational meetings and important decisions. It was here that Greek workers on their own ground chose whether to strike or not, whether or not to support the efforts of the IWW. In 1908 the church also established the Hellenic-American Parochial School to teach and preserve Greek culture and language. This, along with a Sunday School organized in 1910, served to promote and develop Greek consciousness among the children of the community.

By the time of the strike of 1912, the Greeks had firmly established themselves as an important and growing group in Lowell. In twenty years the colony had become a closely-knit cultural unit within the city, numbering 9,000 inhabitants. Serving the community's needs was a small but active middle-class of doctors, retailers, shop and restaurant owners and other small businessmen. Greek workers readily accepted these men as their leaders. When the call for the general strike of textile workers came in 1912, the Greeks were ready. Their experience with other ethnic groups, their community's development, and their conduct in previous strikes prepared them to join in, but as an independent force. This decision to participate in the strike with other nationalities while remaining a distinct group would be important to the success of the workers' demands in 1912. In this way, cultural differences would not fragment the economic interests of textile workers.

EPILOGUE TO LAWRENCE:
THE 1912 STRIKE IN
LOWELL, MASSACHUSETTS

Mary T. Mulligan

Monday, March 25, 1912, marked the start of a four-week strike and lockout in the textile mills of Lowell which would be of local, regional, and, in some respects, national significance. It was the only successful general textile strike in Lowell and the second of at least four consecutive textile strikes in New England led by the Industrial Workers of the World, an attempt by this radical organization to unite the American working class into "One Big Union." The Lawrence strike, the first of its kind in New England, is the one that catapulted the IWW to international fame and is the only one that has received attention. IWW historian, Melvyn Dubofsky, concludes that the Lawrence strike was unique in this region; it alone led to the general wage raise granted throughout the New England textile industry in 1912. Philip S. Foner, in his publication, *The Industrial Workers of the World, 1905-1917*, mentions the strikes at Lowell, Fall River and New Bedford, and admits "other strikes were prevented when the alarmed textile industry decided voluntarily to grant wage increases and other concessions." Yet, Foner comes to the same conclusion that the Lawrence strike caused the regional increase. The Lawrence strike did lead to wage increases, but they were increases determined not collectively, but by the individual mill owners in each textile center. No joint action on the part of the New England owners was taken until the Lowell strike and the threat of further IWW-led strikes in Fall River and New Bedford.

The fact that these strikes were conducted despite the general wage increase indicates that the IWW was not satisfied with the wage gains but was clearly intent upon organizing the textile worker in New England into industrial unions. While historians have neglected the importance of the Lowell strike, the IWW itself regarded its organizational activities in Lowell as even more successful than in Lawrence. The July 4, 1912, issue of the IWW's *Industrial Worker* claimed 20,000 members in Lawrence's Local No. 20 and 28,000 in Lowell's Local No. 436. Coming after the epic, strife-ridden Lawrence struggle, it is understandable why the relatively peaceful Lowell strike in 1912 has been overlooked. Lowell's own historian, Frederick W. Coburn, in his *History of Lowell and Its People* (1920) ignores the 1912 strike, claiming that the city was not affected by the Lawrence strike.

For Lowell, however, this strike, which lasted from March 25 until April 22, 1912, was unprecedented. Its strategy was directed, for the most part, by radical outsiders, known as the Industrial Workers of the World, who organized and advised the mills' unskilled employees, drawn from the recent immigrants from Southern and Eastern Europe. The skilled workers, consisting of English-speaking peoples and a few French-Canadian weavers, were directed by the moderate United Textile Workers Union (UTW), an affiliate of the American Federation of Labor (AFL). The UTW had also been involved in the Lawrence struggle, from which the bitter rivalry over the future of the union movement between the AFL and IWW was extended to the textile centers of the Northeast. This union war was carried over to Lowell. At the first sign that the strike could affect all the mills, the owners responded, as they had in 1903, with a lockout. Throughout the four-week strike period, the city's six major textile mills -- the Appleton, Hamilton, Boott, Tremont & Suffolk, Merrimack, and Massachusetts -- remained closed. This tactic, usually successful against loosely organized or unorganized workers, was not effective against the IWW and UTW in 1912. The workers, both skilled and unskilled, ultimately received a 10% wage advance and other concessions. The strike was won. Its success encouraged militant union activity by the IWW throughout Massachusetts and New England for the remainder of 1912.

The IWW or "Wobblies" as they are more commonly known, was founded in Chicago in the summer of 1905. The founding fathers were Eugene V. Debs, President of the American Socialist Party, and the future leaders of the Lawrence and Lowell strikes,

William D. "Big Bill" Haywood of the Western Federation of Miners, and William E. Trautmann. All reacted against the growth of giant industrial corporations and, what was to them, the ineffectiveness and elitism of the craft unionism of the American Federation of Labor. The IWW encouraged all workers to join industrial unions designed to encompass both the skilled and unskilled workers of either sex, any age, race, ethnic origin or religion, and above all, it "placed ultimate power in the general membership."

Organizational activities of the IWW in the industrial Northeast had begun in May 1908 with a textile workers' convention in Paterson, New Jersey. Among the twenty-two delegates were representatives from the textile centers of Lowell, Lawrence, and New Bedford. The result of this convention was the establishment of the IWW's first national organization, the National Industrial Union of Textile Workers (NIUTW). This industrial union catered to the special needs of the textile worker by providing for subdivisions based on the worker's job function or nationality. Technically, it was the NIUTW which led the 1912 New England strikes.

The most famous IWW strike, and the forerunner of the Lowell conflict, was begun in Lawrence on January 12, 1912, and was not officially ended until March 24. The strike was caused by the wage reduction brought about by the passage of the state's fifty-four hour work law in 1911. This law was designed to reduce the maximum work week for the women and children who worked in the mills, but because it was not feasible to set up two distinct work schedules, mill owners reduced everyone's work week from fifty-six to fifty-four hours per week. In 1909 when the maximum hours for women and children had been reduced from fifty-eight to fifty-six, there had been no wage reduction, and there had been no wage reduction under previous legislation regulating the work week. In early 1912, however, wages were cut an average of thirty cents per week, and the Lawrence strike was on.

National organizer, Joseph Ettor of the IWW, was immediately called in by Lawrence's small Italian IWW local, No. 20. The IWW alone conducted the strike until February 5 and the entrance of the AFL, led by John Golden and the United Textile Workers. Lawrence became divided into two camps: the IWW, which represented the unskilled, foreign-born worker, and the UTW, representing the skilled, native-born workers. The Lawrence strike became not only a war over wages, but also a conflict between rival unions, and each side claimed ultimate victory for the graduated 5% to 17% increase received by all the workers.

Throughout the strike, Lowell kept a watchful eye on the Lawrence situation. The city's two major newspapers, the Democratic *Lowell Sun* and the Republican *Lowell Courier-Citizen*, each provided detailed daily coverage of the strike developments. Their editorials reflected the reaction of the city's propertied interests to the strike, and the newspapers developed a consensus about the Lawrence situation. The *Courier-Citizen* held "very little quarrel with the theory that labor at the present time receives too small a proportion of the wealth created by his hands." The *Sun* proclaimed "their cause just, their course wrong." As an alternative to the strike, the papers advocated the immediate implementation of a nation-wide compulsory arbitration law. Modeled after a Canadian law, this statute would make strikes and lockouts illegal until grievances had been investigated by a government commission. It was their contention that such a law would put a halt to the Lawrence strike by finding in favor of the strikers and thus prevent similar situations from occurring elsewhere.

The Lowell papers maintained that the workers were foolish to strike in the dead of winter and at a time when the Lawrence woolen industry was undergoing "hard sledding." More intelligent operatives, the *Sun* claimed, would have waited for a "more opportune time." The acceptance of IWW leadership by the Lawrence workers was severely criticized. The Lowell press claimed that the union leaders, especially Haywood and Ettor, took advantage of the socialist and violent tendencies inherent in the "Italian and German races," which made up the majority of the Lawrence work force, and as such, formed "an unintelligent class of operatives." Both the *Sun* and *Courier-Citizen* blamed the IWW for the violence which occurred during the Lawrence strike, an accusation which later proved to be groundless. The papers went so far as to place personal responsibility for the violence on Haywood and Ettor. Haywood was portrayed as an "extremist . . . prone to strong-arm tactics . . .," and Ettor as a "trouble-maker . . . [who had] nothing to lose in wrecking the city." The Lowell dailies claimed that the IWW leaders were not out for a settlement, but a widening of the strike, and only in their removal did the papers see a possibility for solution.

After Golden and his AFL-affiliated UTW took an active role in the Lawrence strike, a drastic change took place in the tone of press

Portuguese Mill Girls in the 1912 Strike (Library of Congress)

coverage. The *Sun* hailed his arrival as a "source of satisfaction to
all . . .," which was more a reaction against the IWW than in favor
of the AFL. Both papers had supported the sending of Lowell police
and militia to assist in Lawrence.

After the UTW took a hand in the Lawrence strike and a settlement was still not forthcoming, the Lowell papers began to find
fault with the policies of the mill owners, as well as city officials.
They accused the owners, especially William Wood of the American
Woolen Company, of prolonging needless suffering, when it was
asserted that the mills in Lawrence could afford at least a 10% raise.
City officials were accused of prolonging the strike by their un-
popular efforts to use the police to stop the evacuation of the strikers' children to the homes of sympathizers in other cities. The
Lowell press saw no reason why workers and business both had to
suffer so much, nor why the state had to incur so much expense.

During the Lawrence strike, IWW officials, both there and in
New Bedford, suggested that Lowell would be the scene of their
next strike. Such reports were substantiated by the increased
amount of activity around Matthew Hall at the corner of Central
and Market Streets, the headquarters of Lowell's small IWW chapter, Local No. 436. A substantial amount of money had been collected for the Lawrence relief fund, and weaver Mathias Silva, Secretary of the Portuguese branch of Local 436, reported to the press
that 1,525 Portuguese mill workers had joined the IWW and that
500 more were expected to do the same. The IWW expanded its Portuguese organization in Lowell by sending five Portuguese speakers from Lawrence, who spoke on the strike and enlisted members
for Lowell's chapter from among the 125 Portuguese operatives in
attendance. Actual strike threats came first from "Big Bill" Haywood, and later from "one of the most radical speakers ever heard
in the city," IWW leader, Elizabeth Gurley Flynn, who "talked
strike in vigorous terms." However real and menacing the strike
threats were, the *Sun* and *Courier-Citizen* each dismissed them
lightly.

The newspapers claimed that there were important differences
between the two cities which would more than compensate for any
IWW inroads into Lowell and that the IWW would not be success-
ful in "disturbing industrial conditions outside of Lawrence."
Lowell's industry was based on cotton textiles, not woolens (as in
Lawrence), but the papers claimed there was a more fundamental

difference -- a sociological, even "racial" one. Lawrence mill operatives were reported by the newspapers to be Italian and German,
who they believed to be naturally "socialist." Lowell, the press
argued, had no numerically-dominant class of immigrant worker,
but an entire working populace which was considered "more intelligent and law-abiding" than that of Lawrence, and, as such, would
not succumb to the IWW. These sentiments were echoed by
Redmond Welch, Superintendent of the Lowell Police, as well as by
mill officials.

Even more important was the city's attitude toward its foreign-
born residents. Here, too, Lowell was seen as superior to Lawrence.
The city of Lawrence, characterized by its "greedy landlords and
inept tenement house commissions . . .," caused workers to live in
areas conducive to "not only disease, but socialism." In sharp contrast, Lowell was portrayed in the press as a city anxious to improve
the plight of all her workers, native and foreign. While agreeing
that conditions in Lowell were less than ideal, the press stressed the
philanthropy of the mill owners. In particular, the papers emphasized their voluntary support of a hospital, a public reading room,
special schools to prepare the worker for U.S. citizenship, night
classes at the Lowell Textile Institute, and various religious organizations. The *Courier-Citizen* claimed that actions like these lowered
most of the barriers between the city's native and foreign elements.
Specifically, the French-Canadians had "entered fully into our
civic life . . .;" the Greek was "even becoming naturalized and is
ready to join with us in any patriotic work;" the Pole was now
"inviting contact with the Americans, . . . reading their newspapers,
. . . complimented when recognition is given to his religious or fra-
ternal efforts;" and, as for the Portuguese, "English-speaking
people assisted them in their bazaars . . . [and] invite their participation in the national holidays." Ironically, these four nationalities
were to play dominant roles in the Lowell strike.

One Lowell mill owner raised what was viewed as the ultimate
barrier to an IWW-led strike by announcing on March 11, 1912,
that a wage increase was to go into effect on March 23. This raise,
arranged to coincide with that granted in Lawrence, was given in
anticipation of a demand for wage increases, although, according
the the *Sun*, "many of the mills find it difficult to run at a reasonable
profit." This very increase, hailed as an "act of simple justice that
forestalls any attempt by outside agitators to foment discord . . .,"
was the catalyst for the Lowell strike.

The voluntary wage increase by the Lowell mills, which was in fact *less* than the average wage increase adopted by the textile industry after Lawrence, was the chief issue, but the strike's roots went much deeper. They were embedded in the living and working conditions prevalent in the city. Regardless of local claims of how superior Lowell was to Lawrence, the standard of living among her mill workers was low.

The agent of the Massachusetts Mills, William S. Southworth, maintained that workers avoided mill housing because "they felt themselves a little too good to live in a corporation house." Consequently, the Boott and Massachusetts Mills had provided no housing for their operatives since the turn of the century. The Appleton, Hamilton, Merrimack and Tremont & Suffolk Corporations owned just a few tenements. Therefore, the bulk of the mill operatives, mainly recent immigrants, had to lease from private owners, who charged exorbitant rents for dilapidated housing in areas which were breeding grounds for tuberculosis. Though high for the type of housing, rent consumed only approximately 25% of the average worker's earnings. However, the remainder of his meager salary could barely cover the high cost of living in Lowell. In 1911 prices for food, fuel and clothing in Lowell were equal to, or above, the prices in New York City.

Unable to adequately support a wife and children, the unskilled operative was caught in a vicious circle. The way to earn enough money was to have several family members employed in the mills. However, the larger the number of small children in the family, the more expensive were life's bare essentials: shelter, clothing and food. Once his children left the home to go out on their own, the worker's capacity to earn decreased, leaving him as badly off as before. It is, therefore, easy to comprehend why two or more immigrant families crowded into a one-family apartment, or why workers left their families in the "old country" until they had saved enough money to send for them.

The Irish were the first of what Frederick W. Coburn called the "alien races". This group was later undercut by the French-Canadians, who were, in 1912, under pressure from the Greeks, Poles, and others. Lowell in 1912 numbered among its 120,000 population some 8,000 Greeks. The Market Street area of Lowell was the third-largest colony of Greeks in the United States, surpassed only by New York and Chicago. The factories of Lowell employed more Greeks than were employed anywhere else in the country. Concentrated in the run-down Market Street section of the Acre, Greeks lived in the same dilapidated housing as the other immigrants before them, but by being one of the newest and most organized nationalities in the mills, the Greeks were to play a unique role in the 1912 strike.

All operatives faced the same industrial conditions. Work in the Lowell cotton mills was characterized by long hours, short pay, and health hazards. In 1912 wages averaged around $9.00 per week for the unskilled operative and $15 per week for the highly-skilled worker. Prior to January 1, 1912, the work week was fifty-six hours; after January 1, fifty-four.

All mill workers were prone to respiratory ailments from breathing in the cotton fibers. In 1910 alone, the Lowell Corporation Hospital admitted 761 mill workers, the majority of whom suffered from some lung ailment. Sanitary conditions in the mills were not good, and the fact that most of Lowell's mills operated under a system of absentee ownership did little to alleviate the situation. Those who received the dividends were not acquainted with the actual working conditions in their factories. Of a total of sixty-three directors of the city's six major cotton mills in 1912, only six were Lowell residents. John Jacob Rogers, in addition to being the Director of his own Tremont & Suffolk Mills, looked after the local interests of Arthur T. Lyman's Merrimack and Massachusetts Mills and the Bigelow Carpet Company. Joining him in the city were his son-in-law, F. E. Dunbar, President of the Boott and Appleton Mills; Jude C. Wadleigh, Agent for the Merrimack Manufacturing Company and President of the Textile Agents' Association; Charles F. Young, Treasurer of the Tremont & Suffolk Mills; Alexander Cumnock, Appleton Mills Treasurer; and Frederick Flather, Boott Mills Treasurer.

In the past, mill workers had struck for improvements in their working conditions, but had, on the average, been unsuccessful. According to a local observer in 1911, "of the strikes in Lowell, about one-fifth have been won by the employees, one-fifth have been amicably settled, and three-fifths have been lost ..." The owners met almost every strike -- or threat of one -- with a lockout, and confronted with this, the mill workers, who were generally not very well organized, conceded defeat.

Building on this legacy of worker disorganization, Lowell mill owners on March 11, 1912, announced a wage hike, supposedly

designed to equalize the pay scales in Lowell and Lawrence. The
details of this increase were not posted, however, until Monday
morning, March 25. The proposed increase ranged from 6% to 8%,
less than the 10% granted in Lawrence; workers claimed it was
more of a 4% to 7% offer. As it was less than the increases offered in
the other New England textile centers, this offer was immediately
denounced by the majority of the local IWW members as an attempt
by the Lowell mill officials to gain a competitive advantage at the
expense of their workers. Most of the membership in Local 436,
which hovered around 2,000, was Portuguese and Lithuanian, and
because they made up the majority of the 1,300 employees at the
Appleton Mills, this factory was the first affected. The Appleton
officials employed their traditional weapon, the lockout, and declared the mill would remain closed until there existed "a substantial indication of a willingness on the part of the operatives to
accept the increase offered." Rather than acquiesce, the strikers
went to the other mills in an attempt to persuade their operatives to
join the strike. By the end of the day, they had been successful
enough to make the strike general. The owners responded accordingly, and at 9 a.m. on Tuesday, March 26, the lockout of the
Lowell mills also became general.

The owners, however, would not admit they had locked out the
workers, but claimed that because each process of production was
dependent on the other, they had been forced to close simultane-
ously. With approximately 18,000 employed in the mills, it seemed
doubtful that the 2,000 members of IWW Local 436 could cripple
the mills in a strike. The lockout, however, drove many would-be
strikebreakers into the ranks of the IWW. With this help from the
mills, Local 436 immediately began to organize. Wires were sent to
Lawrence, requesting the assistance of IWW leaders. Trautmann,
Gurley Flynn and Haywood came quickly. They also established
picket lines and appointed a general strike committee. This committee, organized along ethnic lines as in Lawrence, consisted of three
Greeks, five Portuguese, four Lithuanians, four Poles, three Belgians, and two French-Canadians. Thus, it reflected the diverse
makeup of the mills' employees. The three Greek appointees later
withdrew, and, as in 1903, this nationality was to conduct its own
strike.

Now that the impossible had occurred, both city newspapers
became afraid that the violence which marked the Lawrence strike
would occur in Lowell. They renewed their insistence that workers
should get more pay but that strikes were unwise and counseled

the use of arbitration. Both were surprised and grateful that the
first speech of the strike, given on March 26 by IWW organizer,
William E. Trautmann, to a body of strikers on the South Common,
was "much less inflammatory than the ones in Lawrence." They
hailed the closing of the mills as the best possible approach; for organizational reasons, Trautmann hailed it too. The press maintained that the closed mills would reduce the potential for violence,
dampen strike enthusiasm, and limit the flow of strike funds that
the IWW so desperately needed. Trautmann contended that the
shutting down of the mills cut off all profits for the owners, and
thus was "the first step to a worker victory."

The IWW demanded a 15% wage increase for all employees,
double pay for overtime, the right of weavers to weigh their own
cloth for true weight, and the reinstatement of all workers without
discrimination. These demands, very similar to those of the Lawrence strikers, were drawn up by the strike committee, submitted
for approval to the general membership, and then to the mill
owners. The demands were taken to the mill agents by committees
of five, representing the major nationalities present at each mill.
The committees were made up of Portuguese, Poles, Lithuanians,
Armenians, Turks, Syrians, Belgians, French-Canadians, and a few
Americans, English and Irish. Trautmann made it very clear that
these men were not representatives of the IWW national organization, but of the mills' own employees. He maintained that the IWW
was acting solely in an advisory capacity and was not even
demanding recognition. The mill officials, however, saw these committees as representatives of the IWW and harbingers of socialism
and refused to give in to their demands.

John Connell, Agent of the Tremont & Suffolk Mills, said he
would "close them down for a year rather than recognize the
IWW," and Agent Edward W. Thomas, spokesman for the Boott
Mills, refused to meet with the delegates. For the mills, the IWW
represented social revolution. The owners made it known that they
would, however, deal with committees of their mill employees who
were *not* affiliated with the IWW; they meant the craft unions represented by the United Textile Workers. This announcement
caused a sudden increase of activity among the skilled workers --
the loomfixers, mule spinners, and cotton weavers -- who had considered themselves innocent victims of the lockout. The mills in
Lawrence had tried to use the same divisive strategy.

In hoping to gain official recognition for the skilled workers'
unions, these AFL affiliates announced that they would confer

with UTW President Golden, who had led the skilled workers in Lawrence and was on his way to Lowell. He arrived on March 29 accompanied by Carl Wyatt, a general organizer for the AFL, and immediately contacted the UTW's chief ally in the 1903 strike, the Lowell Textile Council, now merged with the Lowell Trades and Labor Council. This Council and the UTW passed a joint resolution condemning the IWW as a menace to "our American form of government ... [and] the legitimate trade union movement." Golden and Wyatt maintained that it was the AFL, not the IWW, that won the Lawrence strike, that they accomplished it peacefully, in two weeks, and would do the same in Lowell. They attacked IWW members as intruders and claimed that in Lowell they would "show the aliens ... [and] bring about American conditions." The IWW's official response was to point to the failures of the UTW in twenty-five years of operation in New England and to warn the strikers on the picket lines of UTW infiltrators who counseled the use of violence, which would then be blamed on the IWW. Trautmann declared that the presence of these "oily reformers" only made it more difficult to resolve the situation. Quickly the strike had veered from its original issue of wage rates and now involved the question of the union war: the IWW - UTW fight for supremacy. Nowhere was this more evident than in the personal clash of Haywood and Golden. Golden labelled Haywood a "self-appointed ... self-constructed character assassin." Haywood retaliated by referring to a published booklet, supposedly carrying the seal of the loomfixers' union, entitled "What John Golden has done for the Textile Workers." The booklet consisted of nothing but blank pages.

Despite the low opinion in which the UTW held the IWW, they issued similar strike demands. The loomfixers, mule spinners, and cotton weavers requested a 15% wage increase, time-and-a-half for overtime, abolition of Sunday work, and the rehiring of striking workers without discrimination. Union members of either stripe were in the minority, constituting about 25% of the approximately 18,000 affected by the general lockout. The mill owners refused the UTW demands, as they had those of the IWW. What is significant is that these refusals were submitted in writing, not verbally, thus indicating a move toward unofficial recognition of the UTW. Mill officials claimed that if a 15% increase were granted, Lowell workers would be receiving more than their Lawrence counterparts, and there would be no end to labor trouble. Clearly refusing to raise Lowell wages to meet the Lawrence increase, the mill representatives stated that the offer of March 25 was fair and final. Connell of the Tremont & Suffolk Mills lamented the strike because "a lot of detail is involved in changing schedules, and errors are unavoidable, but if the workers stayed on, things would have been straightened out." The mill officials refused to meet with employees representing either the IWW or UTW and decided to go on with the lockout.

With their hopes for an immediate settlement dashed, the UTW settled into lethargy. In sharp contrast, activity at the IWW headquarters increased so much that the owners of the Mansur Block requested that they vacate their headquarters at Central and Market Streets. The union's rapidly expanding membership, when not on strike duty, congregated at the headquarters and interfered with the business operations of the other tenants. The IWW also wanted quarters farther away from the Market Street Police Station, thereby forcing the police to tie up the city's one patrol car. For $48 per month they leased Higgins Hall at the corner of Market and Hanover Streets. The building, formerly occupied by the Acme Social and Athletic Club, still contained an eighteen-foot boxing ring in the center of the hall from which the IWW conducted their meetings. This building did, however, provide the union with a centrally located office which facilitated the direction of the strike.

Attending meetings, picketing at the all but empty mills, and parading throughout the mill district -- tactics which had worked at Lawrence -- kept the IWW's followers in Lowell busy. Picket lines were generally set up by 6:15 a.m., and the parades were begun by 7:00. These parades, which ranged in size from several hundred to several thousand people, lasted up to two hours. The most common route was up and down Jackson Street, over Market Street to Bridge Street, across the river along Lakeview Avenue to Aiken Avenue, back across the river to Moody Street to Hanover and Higgins Hall. By following this route, the paraders encircled the mill district and bisected the city's central business district, drawing much public attention. The march leaders generally carried the American flag, emblems of their national groups, and the large red IWW banner, while the paraders chanted, "Fifteen per cent," "Join the strikers," and "Don't be a scab."

Any change from this pattern usually involved a concentration of efforts on a particular mill. However, on one of the opening days of the strike, about five hundred strikers "invaded Belvidere" in search of the Andover Street home of Alexander Cumnock, Treasurer of the Appleton Mills, and the Mansur Street residence of Frederick A. Flather, Boott Mills Treasurer. Instead of marching

1912 Strikers marching on Dutton Street with William "Big Bill" Haywood of the I.W.W. (in derby hat) (Library of Congress)

across Bridge Street, the paraders turned up East Merrimack Street to Nesmith Street and into the city's wealthiest residential section.

In 1975 John Rogers Flather recalled observing the march as a boy, and he remembered that his father's chauffeur had directed the striking marchers away from the Flather house to another part of Belvidere. The strikers were satisfied simply to view the stately homes and returned to the mill district via Fairmount and Rogers Streets. Marred only by a rock-throwing incident on the Rogers Street Bridge, this otherwise peaceful demonstration created a great stir. This first attempt to make the strike felt outside of the city's industrial sector was seen as a grave threat to society. The local papers, in labelling it an "invasion," demonstrated the widely-held view that the march symbolized the beginning of an IWW-led social revolution.

For the most part, the workers remained within the confines of the mill district, but their parades took on an added dimension: music. It was not music to soothe the savage beast, but "noise, noise and plenty of it." The IWW incorporated into its band anything -- trumpets, drums, pans -- that would make noise and referred to Lowell as a "manufacturing Jericho." Although these parades were disturbing and impressive as intended, they were not illegal, and the mayor did nothing to stop them.

Picketing and parading did not account for all of the time of the strikers and their leaders. Each nationality was responsible for organizing its own members and submitting progress reports at regular intervals. This delegation of authority to the nationalities allowed IWW leaders more time to devote to widening the union's influence. Within the city, Trautmann concentrated his efforts on the three mills still in operation. Though not strictly cotton mills, the Bigelow Carpet Company, the Waterhead Mills, and the Lawrence Manufacturing Company were textile mills and, therefore, IWW targets. While it never ceased operation, the Bigelow Carpet Company was almost immediately affected by the strike. Approximately 200 weavers affiliated with the UTW struck, as did 150 unskilled operatives. The onslaught of IWW picketers and paraders at the mill gates did not induce all the employees to strike, and, although crippled, the Carpet Company continued to operate. Similar conditions prevailed at the Lawrence Street site of Lowell's corduroy mill, the Waterhead. However, its striking weavers preferred to settle their own grievances and would not affiliate with either union. Their wage demands, however, were basically the same as the strikers: 15%. In the early days of the strike, the Lawrence Manufacturing Company was the scene of intensive IWW activity. The workers in this mill, which manufactured hosiery and had no looms, were contented with the March 25 increase and refused to strike. Having met with no success, the IWW stopped their efforts at this mill, which hummed with activity while the cotton mills stood silent.

IWW leaders did not confine their organizational activities to Lowell during these weeks. A favorite target was the Amoskeag Mills of Manchester, New Hampshire. Speakers were sent there, and the mill workers organized. These mills were reported to be the target of the IWW's next strike. The city abounded with rumors of where the IWW would go next -- Worcester, Fitchburg, New Bedford, and even back to Lawrence.

The young Irish beauty, Elizabeth Gurley Flynn, a native of New Hampshire and a skilled IWW organizer, proved to be the IWW's most effective speaker during the Lowell strike. A regular parade leader and speaker at morning meetings, she made impassioned pleas for ethnic solidarity, chided the Irish for not being active strikers, and vowed they would win "if it takes all summer." She was so effective at enlisting members, it was rumored in the local press that she received twenty cents for each member she recruited. In addition to labelling her as mercenary, the papers ridiculed her under the guise of typographical errors, using "Elizabeth Curley Flynn" and "Elizabeth Burley Flynn." However, Gurley Flynn was the only IWW leader allowed to address a meeting of the Greeks, and the Greeks were regarded as the key to the strike's success.

While some Greek workers walked out in conjunction with the IWW and others served on the first strike committee, the majority of Greeks were not members of the IWW. As they did in 1903, the Greeks conducted their own strike which was supportive of the IWW but was not affiliated with either union. Once the mills shut down, approximately 600 Greek operatives assembled in their church hall and elected a prominent Greek physician, Dr. George A. Demopoulos, to be their leader. Working class Greeks would cooperate with the IWW strike but only through their leader, Dr. Demopoulos. Though Demopoulos did not like the IWW, he alone of all the Greeks attended their meetings. Any strike information which he determined was pertinent to the Greeks was posted outside the Greek community's own little communication center, Chagaruly's drug store at the corner of Market and Suffolk Streets.

Other than this, the Greek strikers received their instructions directly from the doctor. They were told by him to remain within the Greek section of the city, the Acre, not to go near the IWW's Higgins Hall location but to persuade any Greeks still working in the mills' finishing department to strike. Demopoulos advised the Greeks not only to remain apart from the IWW but to be wary of any union. Another Greek physician, Dr. Demosthenes Generales, who counseled cooperation with the UTW, went unheeded.

The reason for these restrictions on Greek activity was clear: they did not want trouble for their community. They would act as a unit and not become divided. Lawrence Greeks had been praised by the Lowell press for playing only a minor role in that strike, and the honor of Lowell's Greeks hinged upon their conduct. Demopoulos believed that the Greek strikers should "stand loyal with the strike as long as it lasts . . . [and] by . . . be[ing] peaceful and avoid-[ing] by all means, the least disturbance . . . victory, respect and the estimation of the public will be ours."

As the 1903 strike had collapsed when the Greeks among others returned to the mills, the IWW's desire to organize this nationality was understandable. Their new headquarters in the heart of the Greek district, however, provided no opportunities for contact as the Greeks were instructed to avoid it, so the IWW requested that Elizabeth Gurley Flynn be allowed to address the Greek strikers. The Greek leadership agreed to the meeting reluctantly and under the conditions that she not advise the Greeks to join the union or to take part in any of its activities. On April 9 some 1,500 enthusiastic Greek operatives crowded into their church hall to hear her speak. It was unprecedented for a woman to address an audience of Greek men gathered together by their community leaders. Gurley Flynn received a resounding ovation, and her speech, translated by Dr. Demopoulos, conformed to his restrictions. She spoke of the low wages and poor conditions in the mills and the city and asked the Greeks: "Are you, the descendants of the original democracy of the world, going to bring your vigor and manhood into this country to be worn out by a few years of work in the mills and living under conditions such as these?" Her concluding remark spoke to the important role of the Greeks and to what the IWW hoped to attain in Lowell. She proclaimed that "the Lowell strike means more than the Lawrence strike because all nationalities have stood together for the common good, and after the strike is over, they will continue to stand together for better, cleaner and healthier conditions in the city of Lowell."

While unmarred by any large-scale violence, the Lowell strike
did have its share of incidents. Police were present along every
parade route and near each picket line. They quickly arrested
anyone who caused a disturbance. Strikers threw rocks at passing
autos on the Rogers Street Bridge, windows were smashed at the
Bigelow Carpet Company, and a small scuffle, requiring additional
police assistance, ensued when striking Poles refused to clear East
Merrimack Street sidewalks. However, these events were atypical.
The majority of arrests came under the headings "illegal picketing"
and "assault on an unknown person," and usually involved a striker's attempt to force a bystander to join the parade or picket line.
The arrested individuals were taken before Judge John J. Pickman
of the Police Court, and fines ranged from $8.00 to $45 depending
upon the severity of the charge.

The IWW usually paid the fine, but when one striker refused to
pay, it created quite a stir in the city. Alice George, a seventeen-year
old Syrian striker, was arrested Monday, April 1, at the Bigelow
Carpet Company on charges of illegal picketing and assault on two
women. Taken before Judge Pickman and fined $8.00, George
maintained she was innocent and refused to pay. She was then
placed under arrest, and bail was set at $200. The Syrians were
often confused with Greeks, and the *Courier-Citizen* had published
a picture of George standing in front of a Greek bakery. Dr. Demopoulos saw her imprisonment as a possible threat to the Greeks'
reputation and took the initiative. He posted bail, advised her to
withdraw her appeal, and paid her fine. George was turned into an
instant celebrity and became the only Syrian and only local female
representative at the strike community meetings.

With little progress and no settlement forthcoming in the immediate future, many operatives sought other alternatives. *L'Etoile*,
the French community's newspaper, published notices that New
Hampshire concerns were looking for weavers, and approximately
seventy-five Belgian weavers found employment in the mills of
Newmarket, New Hampshire. In April there was as big an exodus
back to Canada as during the 1903 strike which, *L'Etoile* claimed,
was not strike-related but an annual occurrence. Reports of French
delegates to the IWW meetings suggested a different explanation.
They reported that members of their nationality were leaving the
city to seek work rather than break the strike. 150 Portuguese, the
most militant nationality, also left the city. Mill officials were not
too concerned with an exodus of easily replaceable unskilled workers. The IWW, however, was deeply disappointed.

The Lowell operatives had received their last paycheck on Friday, March 29, and all three factions in the city -- the IWW, the UTW, and the Greeks -- were faced with providing relief or losing their supporters and the strike. Of the three, the IWW was confronted with the most momentous task. A sensational appeal for aid was sent out to neighboring cities. Capitalizing on the sufferings of the mill worker, it contained such phrases as "a life barren of hope ... denied the pursuit of happiness ... [and] sold out by the vampires on the battlefield of labor." The sending of this appeal, which was seen by the *Courier-Citizen* as "drawn from fancy not fact ... and ... typical of Socialist prose poetry ...," was closely followed by the organization of finance committees. These committees, made up exclusively of women who could attest more readily to family hardships, were sent to surrounding textile centers in an effort to solicit funds. The Lawrence, Fall River, and New Bedford committees met with great success; in an afternoon's work in these textile cities, they collected over $400. The Boston committee met with less success, and the Manchester solicitors met with resistance. They were arrested as a result of a recent ordinance against soliciting by labor representatives and escorted back to the railroad station where they were put on a Lowell-bound train. Unsolicited funds came both from within the city and outside New England. The Lowell Leatherworkers' Union pledged $100 per week until the strike's conclusion, and generous contributions came in from IWW committees in New York, Philadelphia, Baltimore, and Detroit.

Assured of a continuous supply of funds, the IWW set about establishing a relief system, or as they referred to it, a "co-operative program." This program of money and food distribution was conducted discretely; the names of aid recipients were not disclosed. The humiliation of charity was carefully avoided. The Portuguese who remained in the city proved particularly helpful in running this program. A Portuguese baker volunteered free labor and bread to the strikers if the committee would pay for the ingredients, and 463 loaves were distributed the first day. Portuguese delegates also made arrangements for the opening of an IWW grocery store, if conditions warranted it. These IWW efforts to keep mill operatives in the city were available to all workers, but the response was so overwhelming that, for practical reasons, the program was limited to card-carrying IWW members. The UTW-affiliated strikers received financial aid only from the union's national headquarters and the craft unions of New England.

The Greeks, many of whom had left their families in Greece and who were conscientious savers of their weekly earnings, were the least needy of all affected and provided for their own relief. Demopoulos personally solicited funds from the Greek communities of New York and Boston. He arranged for three local committees: one to solicit funds among Greeks in local towns, another to receive these funds and handle them, and the third to investigate the needs of the strikers. The money was not given to the strikers, because Demopoulos maintained "to give anyone too much money when idle, is not good policy," but rather to local Greek merchants to keep their shelves stocked. These goods were to be distributed to the needy, but the Greeks did not find it necessary to utilize this program.

The first breakthrough in the stalemated strike came, not in Lowell, but in other New England textile centers. The management of the Amoskeag Mills of Manchester announced on April 3 a return to the wage scale of 1907, which would result in about a 10% increase in wages. This announcement and similar ones from Fall River and New Bedford, designed to foil IWW inroads in these cities, affected the Lowell situation. The strikers still officially demanded 15%, and the local officials stood firm with the March 25 offer, but as Lowell was the only New England textile center which had not granted at least a 10% wage raise, mill officials were being pressured to concede the full 10% hike, and a compromise seemed likely.

It was at this time that the city government chose to inject itself into the strike. On April 4, Democratic Mayor James E. O'Donnell made his first public move towards achieving a settlement, rumored to have been requested by two mills, one of which had a big order and the other a government contract. The mayor proposed giving the wage increase offered by the mills on March 25 a test run. In a plan similar to one proposed in 1903, the operatives were to return to the mills on April 8 to work for three weeks under the March 25 rates, and, if not satisfied with their wages, resubmit their demands. In the event they were refused again, in O'Donnell's view, the operatives would be justified in stopping work and using arbitration to bring about an adjustment. Copies of this proposal were sent to the mill agents, UTW-affiliates, and Demopoulos, but *not* to the IWW. Mill officials saw this plan only as a postponement of the strike, not as a way of gaining a settlement, so they rejected it. UTW-affiliates rejected it, citing the

10% raises in the rest of New England. In a significant move, Demopoulos let the IWW speak for the Greeks, and they rejected the offer on principle. The general strike committee refused to accept any city interference in the strike and was backed whole-heartedly by the strikers, particularly the Portuguese who, in a public statement, declared "the workers will fight their own battles with their masters."

The mayor and his proposal were soon forgotten. On Saturday, April 6, the Lowell Trades and Labor Council and the UTW reduced their demands from 15% to 10%. On the same day, notice was received of the general 10% raise in all other New England cotton mills and of the censure of the Lowell mill owners by the New England Association of Textile Manufacturers for not raising their wages. These announcements increased the enthusiasm of the Lowell strikers and had a particularly strong effect on the English-speaking skilled operatives. Prior to this, their attitude was one of indifference; but now that success seemed assured, they took an active part in the parades and joined the picket lines.

Jude C. Wadleigh, a representative of the Lowell mill agents and President of the Lowell Manufacturers' Association, said the mills' position would not change, but a suddenly convened meeting of mill agents in Boston pointed to capitulation. Attending this extended session were officials from each of the struck mills: Cumnock of the Appleton Mills; Charles F. Young of the Tremont & Suffolk; Arthur R. Sharp of the Hamilton; Flather of the Boott; and Arthur T. Lyman, President of the Merrimack and Massachusetts Mills. Everyone expected them to concede to a 10% raise. Although still publicly demanding a 15% hike, the IWW made anticipatory preparations. They made it clear they would only consider an offer made either directly to them or to the workers and made arrangements for a mass meeting on the South Common. At this meeting, the strikers would be presented with the mill owners' offer and "decide for themselves as to a settlement." The results of the Boston meeting were officially released on Saturday, April 13, in the following statement by Wadleigh:

> The mills will open Monday, April 22, with an advance in wages on a basis of 10%, over the schedule of wages in force before March 25, 1912.

The Lowell mills had capitulated to the pressure of the industry. This general offer, which included all the struck mills, as well as the Bigelow Carpet Company and the Waterhead Mills, but not the unaffected Lawrence Manufacturing Company, was immediately accepted by both the UTW and the Greeks. The Greek acceptance, though supposedly hinging on the approval of the other nationalities, left the IWW with little choice -- either they could accept this and claim a victory or fight a losing battle for 15%. The strike committee chose to accept the offer, but did so with one reservation:

> Realizing that a continuation of the strike of textile workers in Lowell, with a partial victory already won, would only increase the suffering of thousands who would under no consideration renounce the principles which guided this industrial struggle from the outset, and aware of the fact that over 18,000 textile workers of Lowell, now organized to obtain a larger share of the product they produce, can more successfully enforce their demands in the places of employment and secure redress of wrongs they suffer under, therefore, be it

> RESOLVED: that the strike committee, representing 18,000 men, women, and children recommend that the proposition of the ten per cent flat increase in wages for all employees without exception, be accepted, providing that the other grievances submitted in letters to the employers be adjusted between committees of the employees and their own employers prior to the return of the latter to work on April 22nd.

To insure the mills did not re-open until these grievances had been settled, the IWW continued its policy of parades and picket lines, while the committees of mill employees brought their seven-point letter to the mill officials. Included in this letter were questions concerning overtime pay, discriminatory re-hiring practices, the weaver's right to weigh his own cloth, and the type of increase, whether flat or graduated.

The IWW received satisfactory responses from all the mill agents, except Agent Stephen T. Whittier of the Hamilton Mills. He refused to meet with the committee. Consequently, on Thursday morning, April 18, four hundred strikers reported for picket line duty at the Hamilton Mills. The police, believing the strike to be over, had only assigned six men to the area, and when they tried to arrest a Portuguese man for assault, a riot ensued.

The angry crowd began throwing rocks at both the officers and the mill windows, and the police quickly sent for reinforcements. Even with the additional help, the police had a difficult time controlling the crowd. Nineteen mill windows were broken before one officer fired his revolver in the air, causing a sudden dispersal of the crowd and the end to the only significant violence of the Lowell strike. After a threat by Demopoulos to renew the strike, Whittier agreed to meet with his employees and responded satisfactorily to all their demands.

The IWW strike committee voted to end the strike, and Saturday, April 20, was set aside for the meeting on the South Common and the victory parade. In addition to the 10% raise, the 10,000 paraders, including 2,000 from Lawrence, were celebrating the granting of time-and-one-quarter for overtime, the right for a weaver to weigh his own cloth, and the re-hiring of all workers without discrimination. True to form, the Greeks held their own parade, over 3,000 strong, but did take part in the South Common meeting, where the amassed strikers voted, resoundingly, to accept the offer and return to the mills on Monday, April 22. On that day, and without incident, Lowell's newspapers headlined "GREAT COTTON MILLS STARTED UP AFTER MONTH'S IDLENESS."

The Lowell strike was considered by the *Sun* and *Courier-Citizen* in much the same vein as they had viewed the Lawrence struggle. When their plea to the strikers for arbitration went unheeded, the papers gave their support to the mill owners and the March 25 offer. The operatives, they claimed, should be the ones to concede. They advocated consideration of the mayor's proposal but radically altered their position when news came of the UTW's 10% demand and the general New England wage increase. Both papers then criticized management for their stubbornness and called for the granting of a 10% raise. The operatives, they feared, "will remain out for months unless they get some concession." The papers also feared, as their headlines stated, the implementation of "More Aggressive Tactics," and that "The Exodus of Skilled Help Will Ruin The Factories." The announcement of the increase was met with mixed emotion. Grateful that the 10% was finally granted, they were also critical of the week-long delay. The *Sun* and *Courier-Citizen* again were both more anti-IWW than pro-UTW. The IWW was blamed for the violence that did occur although the lack of major disturbances was credited to the effectiveness of the police.

Adding a third dimension to the strike coverage was the city's French-language paper, *L'Etoile*. This Republican-oriented paper restricted its coverage to factual reporting. Its strike-related editorials were limited to the strike's opening days. The paper advocated peaceful means to achieve a settlement, and above all, did not want any Franco-Americans to be connected with violence. This advice reflected a policy similar to that of the Greeks. Lowell's French-Canadian residents had put forty years of hard, honest work into achieving their good reputation in the community, and the paper wanted it maintained.

The Lowell strike provided Lawrence newspapers with a chance to get even. The Lawrence press, taking exception to Lowell's earlier claim to superiority, contended that Lowell was saved only by the closing of the mills and would profit from Lawrence's experiences, a statement which came true. The Lawrence press did admit to differences in the two cities but only in regard to the role of the Greeks, which even they saw as significant. They naturally compared the Lowell strike with their own, and this was reflected in their coverage. At the onset of the strike, the four papers -- *The Evening Tribune, The Lawrence Daily American*, the *Lawrence Sun*, and the *Lawrence Telegram* -- gave a considerable amount of space to the events in Lowell. However, next to Lawrence's violence, the relatively peaceful Lowell strike seemed disappointingly dull, and the amount of coverage decreased daily until only small articles heralded its conclusion. Apparently, they viewed it solely as a poor copy of their own strike.

The Lowell strike signified more than the 10% wage increase. The strike and subsequent lockout did cause the emigration of many city residents. The mill owners brought any loss of profit upon themselves with the lockout, and the workers, though losing approximately $400,000 in wages, gained the opportunity to improve both their wages and working conditions. One of the last actions by the IWW prior to the strike's conclusion was the organization of shop committees. These committees, welcomed by the owners as an alternative to strikes, were made up of each mill's own employees and were to be the intermediaries between the workers and owners. Any grievances were first to be taken to the mill's shop committee. If the committee felt the complaint was justified, it would relay it to the proper mill official. How long the committees lasted or how effective they were is not known, but their mere organization is significant.

The end of the strike terminated the role of Dr. Demopoulos in labor activities. His firm leadership won a dual victory for the Greeks: a 10% raise and community respect. The *Sun*, echoing the sentiments of the community, commended the Greek strikers for their moderation. Golden and the UTW left Lowell as quickly as did the IWW leadership.

IWW activity in Lowell, however, continued throughout 1912. A brief, unsuccessful strike by IWW weavers at the Appleton Mills began on September 3, and ended on September 7. This strike was ill-advised. The weavers' central demand was for a closed shop which would involve firing the mills' ninety non-IWW employees. A Massachusetts Open Shop Law of 1909 made it illegal for a worker to be forced into joining a union or discriminated against because he or she did not belong. Rather than face prosecution under the law for what was an isolated incident, the strikers relented and returned to the mill.

The strikes in Lowell, Lawrence and throughout New England were the highpoint in IWW history in the industrial Northeast. Though Lawrence rocketed the IWW to international fame, the Lowell victory and the push to organize Fall River and New Bedford added momentum to its cause. The IWW bandwagon came to a screeching halt, however, with the failure of the 1913 textile strike in Paterson, New Jersey, which ironically was the site of their first inroads into the Eastern textile industry. Having come full circle in the East, the union after 1913 shifted back to its Western interests. Suspected of treasonable activity during World War I and hounded for its opposition to the war by the federal government, the IWW declined steadily in both power and influence. Although no longer an effective force after 1920, the Industrial Workers of the World is not defunct nor forgotten. The heyday of this union came in the Merrimack Valley, and Lawrence should not receive all the credit nor the blame. Lowell also played a role, a significant one.

WORLD WAR I AND THE
1918 COTTON TEXTILE STRIKE

by Edward J. Scollan

The 1918 cotton textile strike in Lowell was brief. It began on Monday, July 1, 1918, with the refusal of mill owners to grant a full 15% wage increase to cotton mill operatives. Negotiation and arbitration followed, and the mill owners finally agreed to the original 15% demand of the operatives. Strikers then returned to work in full force on July 8, 1918. Unlike Lowell's 1912 textile strike, the 1918 cotton textile strike was conservative. It espoused no real change in the relationship of labor and management, and no incidents of unrest or mass protest were reported by the two local newspapers. John Golden, who as President of the United Textile Workers (American Federal of Labor) came to Lowell to organize the strike, was opposed to militant confrontation. The 1918 cotton textile strike was not a movement for better working conditions, for shorter hours, or for the right to union organization. The strikers had only one demand--a 15% wage increase.

Lowell operatives were not alone in their desire to receive higher pay. Workers in other mill towns in Massachusetts also demanded wage increases. By the year 1918 the United States was fully tied, both economically and militarily, to the Allied cause in Europe. The American economic relationship to the European war had produced a time of great prosperity at home. Unemployment was virtually eliminated, and the increased demand for skilled and unskilled labor raised wages slowly but steadily in all industries. In cotton manufacturing, which was one of the lowest paying industries, the average hourly wage rose from 15.3 cents an hour in

1914 to 15.8 cents an hour in 1916, but by the beginning of 1918, the hourly wage had jumped to 26.7 cents. The increases in the hourly rates looked impressive, but in most cases they were eaten up by the high cost of living. The stable output of civilian goods with the increase in purchasing power produced a marked inflationary spiral, and real wages just barely kept pace with the cost of living. The Relative Cost of Living Index, nationwide, rose 70% between December 1914 and December 1918. This increase offset a substantial part of wage advances prior to 1918.

World War I also increased the productivity of manufacturing. The increase in industrial capacity led to changes in production methods. The institution of the double-shift routine in factories and textile mills led to an even greater output. With no government price controls, many companies were able to make enormous profits during World War I. For most corporations and textile mills, profits increased rapidly until the government imposed higher corporation taxes in 1918 and 1919.

The economic situation of Lowell in 1918 reflected the general trend in the country. The boom in textile manufacturing because of increased government contracts with total U.S. involvement in the war had created a scarcity of labor in the Lowell area. There was an organized effort by textile managers to keep those already working in Lowell on the job, but also to attract more operatives to the Lowell mills. Full page advertisements in the *Lowell Courier-Citizen* in January 1918, sponsored by the American Woolen Corporation and the Lowell Cotton Manufacturing Association along with over thirty other factories and business establishments, propagandized the benefits of working in Lowell. The ads read: "Pay envelopes are well filled in Lowell these days . . ." for workers in factories with the newest in technology and safety devices. This effort by the business community to keep workers from moving away and to bring new labor into the area was soon reflected in newspaper editorials praising Lowell and the chances of success in the community. In March the *Citizen* rejoiced over the economic prosperity in Lowell. But it made its position clear with regard to the behavior of Lowell operatives in their new-found affluence. They must be "worthy of employment" and "willing to stick to the job" to receive a fair share of this new prosperity.

Indeed, Lowell was prosperous during the war, but as in other textile cities most of the wages earned by textile workers were needed to combat inflation and the high cost of living.

For example, milk prices rose by 37%, cornmeal by 77%, and bacon by 64% between January 1917 and January 1918. Many workers, both inside and outside the textile industry, sought advances in real wages. The common attitude that prevailed in many of the workers' and operatives' minds was that they too should receive a fair share of the country's new war-time wealth.

Prior to the strike in July 1918, there were a number of demands for wage advances in Lowell. Most were settled before a strike took place. The majority of these incidents involved only a call for increased pay and lasted briefly. Demands came from telephone operators, painters, bartenders, and municipal employees, one following the other, seeking increases of 10%, 15%, or even 25% in wages. In just about all cases, the workers got some increase. They concentrated on "bread and butter" issues and on no other demands. Wages and prices were rising, and everyone wanted to receive a real share of the prosperity.

Both of Lowell's daily newspapers, the *Lowell Sun* and the *Lowell Courier-Citizen* provided information on local, state, and national labor problems. Besides news stories, both carried editorials on labor, wages, strikes or possible strikes, and their relationship to the American effort to win the war. In the spring of 1918 the conservative, Republican *Courier-Citizen* constantly attacked the idea of a strike during war-time and sided with management's position on labor. Labor must be willing to "enlist in the war." The *Citizen* questioned the loyalty of anyone who favored strikes. Strikes in war-related industries, such as textiles or munitions, were simply "intolerable and unpatriotic." Day after day, editorial after editorial, the paper reminded its readers that the "country is at war and we cannot act as if the time were one of profound peace." Strikes or labor disputes were delays, and "every hour of delay, especially in wage disputes. . . is like a stab in the back of our armies." The editorial policy played on the operatives' patriotism. It hoped to make strikers or future strikers feel unpatriotic about striking during the war. Judging by the number and frequency of labor disputes in the Lowell area, this editorial policy was unsuccessful.

The Democratic *Lowell Sun*, although no champion of workers' rights, took a more moderate position on the labor situation. The war needed the loyal support of all citizens to be carried out successfully. The *Sun* hoped labor disputes could be settled quickly with "arbitration [as] the best method." Work should continue because of its urgency to the war situation. But if arbitration did fail, strikes must be ended at all costs. The *Sun* agreed with the *Citizen* that "strikes aid the enemy," but was convinced that "labor, generally throughout the country, is now cooperating loyally with the Government in its war work." The *Sun* editor felt that "labor is apparently doing its duty in this war of democracy in spite of the strikes which occasionally occur."

On Thursday, March 14, 1918, local newspapers announced that a wage advance in the local cotton mills would take place on April 1. This increase was reportedly a 10% increase in the cotton operatives' pay scale. The raise would affect approximately 18,000 operatives in Lowell's cotton mills with the lowest paid workers benefiting the most. The *Citizen* reported that from 1916 to 1918, local cotton operatives had obtained 67% in wage increases. It praised the mill agents for granting the increase because it showed that Lowell was no "longer a low wage community." All the mills giving the pay raise were engaged in heavy government production.

Less than two months later on June 5, the skilled cotton operatives led by the United Textile Workers sought an additional 15%. The union insisted that the increase take effect on June 17. The American Woolen Corporation, a holding company which owned several mills in the Greater Lowell area, answered that they would be willing to grant an advance, but not 15%. They proposed that a 10% raise in wages go into effect on June 17. The *Sun* found it "gratifying to find that the local mill corporations granted an increase of ten percent in wages without much haggling." Furthermore the *Sun*, again the more moderate of the local papers, pointed out that many of the mills were engaged in government production and were "doubtless earning good profits . . . ." The *Citizen* saw the increase as simply one more in an endless chain. It stated that wages had risen 77% since the beginning of the war, and "it may be difficult to get up very much ardent sympathy with the demands for still more . . . ." The *Citizen* reminded the operatives that wages would not stay high and that they must prepare for decreases in pay once the United States was victorious in Europe. The union stuck to the original 15% demand. Under the leadership of John Golden and the United Textile Workers, the cotton textile operatives of Lowell were willing to strike for the 5% difference.

In 1918 the majority of skilled workers in Lowell's cotton textile industry belonged to the United Textile Workers. The UTW began its first drive to organize skilled operatives in the cotton manufacturing industry in 1901. Loomfixers, mule spinners, and weavers were moulded into independent craft organizations which used a federation of crafts (UTW) to protect their self-interest. The UTW was conservative in its outlook, seeking gains for skilled workers. From the beginning, the UTW had problems with organizational strategy and with rivals which also sought to represent the textile operatives. An example of ineffective strategy was the 1903 strike in the Lowell cotton mills. In 1918, John Golden of the UTW, would make it a point to emphasize, again and again, that this strike, unlike the 1903 strike, was for all cotton operatives, both skilled and unskilled.

After 1903 two separate organizations challenged the United Textile Workers. Competition from the right was led by the National Amalgamation of Textile Operatives, which in 1916 broke with the UTW. This break is significant because it marked the failure of the UTW to hold the allegiance of all craft organizations in the New England cotton mills. Competition from the left also reduced UTW membership before the war. The Industrial Workers of the World, or "Wobblies," had been gaining strength which would culminate in the successful Lawrence strike of 1912. The IWW, unlike the UTW, concentrated on workers left out of the skilled unions. After the Lawrence strike of 1912, both the IWW and the UTW moved to Lowell to continue their competition for the support of textile workers. By 1918, however, only the United Textile Workers remained to organize a successful strike.

When the mill agents refused to grant the extra 5% increase demanded by the UTW in July 1918, Golden announced that a strike vote would be taken. On Saturday, June 29, the headlines proclaimed that the "Lowell Cotton Mill Operatives Strike." The strike would begin on Monday, July 1, unless the additional 5% demand was met. Golden stated that the strike would affect seven mills and approximately 18,000 workers. Even before the strike was officially declared, the *Citizen* began its editorial attack. It suggested that it was "time for a warning note" to the operatives. Industry "must not be bribed" to do its duty to help win the war.

Golden and the UTW presented their case to the public. The UTW defended the demand for a wage increase, suggesting that the mills were making large profits from the war and that Lowell could well afford the additional 5% increase in wages. He added that if they refused, the members of the UTW were numerous enough to cripple the cotton mills. Golden claimed that Lowell was a well organized union community and that everything would be done to achieve success. Unlike the 1912 textile strike, this strike consisted of only one "bread and butter" economic demand.

The mill agents responded quickly. They emphasized that increases in Lowell's cotton mill wages totaled 95% in the last two years. Agent J.C. Wadleigh of the Merrimack Manufacturing Company in a letter to the Lowell Textile Council indicated that it would be impossible for the mills to grant an increase. Substantial wage advancements had been handed out in the past, but now the mills could no longer afford the increases.

Cotton operatives in Lowell were almost fully organized by 1918. But only 25% of those with UTW membership were skilled workers in the positions of loomfixers, slasher-tenders, beamers, and weavers. Although relatively small in number, these positions were important in production because of the interdependence of departments in mill production. Without the full employment of the skilled workers, the UTW believed that production would be held at a standstill. Golden hoped that these skilled workers could effectively stop or slow-down mill operations during the strike. So although it was a general UTW strike, the most important operatives for the UTW to keep away from mill production were the skilled workers. On the first day of the strike the newspapers reported that 70% of the work force, mostly unskilled operatives, showed up for work. Golden issued a call for solidarity, insisting that "this is not a strike of one department or one union, but a strike of the United Textile Workers of America." Each worker, skilled or unskilled, is of equal importance in the effectiveness of the strike, he said. Golden's strategy was to rely on the impact of withholding the skilled, but organizing the unskilled for solidarity.

The UTW established picket lines in front of those companies affected by the strike: the Massachusetts Mills, the Boott Mills, the Tremont and Suffolk Mills, along with the Appleton and Hamilton Mills. The conservative nature of the UTW and its conduct in the Lowell strike was clear. From the outset of the strike, John Golden spoke again and again of the peaceful intentions of the UTW. The United Textile Workers sought success by argument rather than force and by convincing the Lowell public that the strike would continue along "smooth lines." Golden assured the community that the radical and unpatriotic Industrial Workers of the World would have no part in the organization of the Lowell strike in 1918.

The second day of the strike brought both federal and state government representatives to Lowell to confer with the mill agents and the operatives. Successful organization techniques secured more support for the strike even from the non-union textile workers, and an effective walkout occured. Only 30% of the cotton operatives reported to work on July 2, holding production to a minimum. Since the demand was only for a wage increase, both federal and state authorities were confident of a quick settlement. Henry J. Skeffington, U.S. Commissioner of Immigration to the Port of Boston, and J. Walter Mullen of the Massachusetts State Board of Arbitration arrived in Lowell on July 2. Skeffington was commissioned by the federal government to assist in the settlement of labor troubles in the Eastern States, and both Skeffington and Mullen met with Golden to listen to the official demands of the UTW. Skeffington hoped for a quick settlement in the strike. In addition to the Lowell cotton strike, there were labor disturbances reported in three of the largest New England textile centers, Manchester, New Hampshire and Pawtucket and Woonsocket, Rhode Island.

The UTW and the mill agents disagreed over who would be in charge of arbitration. Both were willing to submit their differences to an arbitration board but not to the same one. The mill treasurers favored the National War Labor Board because all decisions it had handed down included the stipulation that there would be no more strikes for the duration of the war. All future labor disputes would have to be submitted to arbitration while production continued. Even if the NWLB came to Lowell and found in favor of the operatives, it would prohibit all future cotton textile strikes in the community. The mill agents would be willing to sacrifice this additional 5% because all future labor troubles would have to go to the NWLB. During this arbitration, the operatives would be compelled to continue production, thus losing the strike as an effective weapon.

The National War Labor Board was formed in 1916 by President Woodrow Wilson to prevent labor disputes in war-related industries. The board, representing both labor and management, operated by means of conciliation and mediation. It recommended that all strikes and lockouts be avoided during the war, but that the right to organize for union recognition not be denied. The National War Labor Board did not have any enforcement powers to compel employers or employees to abide by its decisions, but it carried the force of the Wilson Administration behind it.

On July 2, the mill treasurers sent a telegram to Secretary of War, Newton D. Baker, with the hope that he would suggest the National War Labor Board be sent to Lowell to end the strike. The mill agents believed that since the majority of textile production was involved with government contracts, the NWLB should be responsible for the strike's arbitration. This request was denied on July 5 by Secretary Baker, who stated that the NWLB was used mainly in strikes when all other methods of arbitration had failed. In a letter to the Executive Manager of the Massachusetts State Committee on Public Safety, Henry B. Endicott, Baker suggested that Endicott use his office to settle the Lowell strike. This ended all hopes that the NWLB would come to Lowell.

The strike was now in its third day. Daily production was reduced to almost nothing with only a small percentage of unskilled and skilled operatives reporting to work. The *Citizen* increased its attack on the strikers, suggesting the possibility of German influence behind this and other strikes. It cautioned the public to be alert because there was "often a German in the wood-pile." Although the individual striker was an "innocent cog" in the strike machinery, there was a strong possibility the strike was being organized by German sympathizers. The *Citizen* also questioned the value of professional labor leaders. Under the new work or fight law enacted by the Congress, one had to be engaged in a "useful" occupation or be subject to conscription. The *Citizen* believed that Golden was not employed in any worthwhile occupation, and an editorial on July 3 asked the question: is John Golden doing his part to win the war? It suggested Golden follow the actions of Samuel Gompers, President of the AFL, who publicly announced that labor should refrain from strikes during war-time.

Golden responded by defending the UTW and the operatives' demands. Patriotism could not be used as an issue against the UTW, he said. The UTW and its members had donated large sums of money to the Liberty Bond Campaign and the Red Cross, not to mention the large number of men sent to the European front. The reasons for the requested wage increase included the high cost of living, increased rents, and the high inflation rate in the Lowell area. Although the mill agents claimed that wages had increased by 95%, Golden reminded the public that the inflation rate had also increased by 93%. Wages paid in Lowell were still below those in surrounding mill towns.

After Lowell's July 4 celebration during which all the mills closed down, the Endicott State Arbitration Board arrived in

Lowell. The mill agents now agreed to submit to arbitration by this board instead of the National War Labor Board. The main concern of the mills, along with the local papers, was to return to maximum war production. At first the *Citizen* attacked Endicott and the board. Like the mill agents, the *Citizen* believed that the strike was of concern to the war effort and should be arbitrated accordingly. The *Citizen* hoped that this would be the last strike by operatives in Lowell, the main reason it had preferred the NWLB. The paper had attacked Endicott as a "walking Christmas tree," but quickly shifted its position to support the mill agents' acceptance of arbitration.

On July 5 both sides agreed to submit to arbitration, and a meeting was held with the Endicott Arbitration Board. The board allowed each group to speak in the debate on the wage increase. Agent William A. Mitchell of the Massachusetts Mills represented the management's interests. He spoke at the meeting, stressing the many increases that had already been granted to the Lowell operatives. He used as examples the wages of skilled workers, citing a slasher-tender who in 1916 started at $11.30 per week, but was now making $24.17 per week, an increase of 114%. Loomfixers jumped from $12.90 per week in 1916 to the current rate of $27.22 per week, an increase of 111%. Mitchell concluded that the mills could simply not afford to grant additional advances. Golden, in response, noted that although the figures looked impressive, other factors must be taken into consideration. These figures were still below the normal level of wages paid in other communities such as Fall River and New Bedford. Golden also summoned up the spectre of the IWW, reminding the board that the strike led by the UTW had been peaceful. He did not discuss the wages of unskilled workers.

The meeting was brief and then adjourned, enabling Endicott to make his decision. By now both newspapers wanted the operatives to return to work and hoped for a quick decision by the arbitration board. As the *Sun* put it, the extra 5% increase was "a small bone of contention" to hold up production. Endicott agreed, and late on July 5 he ruled in favor of the operatives. But the award was hardly a victory for the strikers. It contained a clause that prohibited strikes for the duration of the war stating that, "there shall be absolutely no interruption of the production of the textile mills of Lowell so long as the war shall last." This is exactly what the mill agents had hoped for. This would insure a continual flow of production in Lowell's textile industry. Any future disputes would be submitted to the National War Labor Board, and they in turn would either hear the case or assign it to a proper authority.

The second part of the Endicott decision granted the 15% increase to the strikers. This was the original 10% offer by the mill agents, plus the extra 5% sought by the operatives. Endicott found that, considering the overall cost of living in Lowell, the strikers' demand for an increase in wages was warranted. The increase was made retroactive to June 17, the date of the initial demand. Both Golden and the representatives of mill interests agreed to abide by the board's ruling. They hoped that a majority of operatives could return to work on Saturday, but full production would begin on Monday morning.

The *Sun* hailed the agreement as fair and satisfactory to each side. Since there would be no more strikes essential war work could continue without interruption. The *Citizen*, although satisfied with the Endicott decision, still issued warnings to the operatives. They must abide by the clause which prohibited strikes during war-time and insisted that all future disputes be quickly submitted to the National War Labor Board. But the paper went one step further. Why should strikes be prohibited only during war-time? Serious consideration should be given to ending *all* strikes, war or no war. Arbitration should be used to settle any and all differences.

The Lowell newspapers' increasingly hostile attitude towards labor with regard to strikes should be put into perspective. Both July and August were important months in the Allied war effort. After a lengthy stalemate, American and French Armies were winning significant victories on the Western Front. By reading both papers, one gets the feeling that each sensed an Allied victory in the air. Because of this, they were determined not to let labor interfere with the war effort. Their main concern was to keep labor at an optimal level of output. A concession here or there was allowable, so long as production continued. The Lowell strike of 1918 was a strike with no major labor demands other than wages. The country's war-time economic prosperity had seemed to erase concern for shorter hours, better working conditions or union organization from the operatives' minds. The main concern was wages, but higher wages in an uncontrolled war-time economy inevitably led to more inflation, an endless cycle that would end only with the collapse of the war boom. Considering the potential power that labor had in 1918, little was accomplished by the UTW, and the vital weapon of the strike was bargained away for a 5% wage increase.

THE LOWELL SHOE STRIKE IN 1933

by Edward Rocha

The cotton textile industry in Lowell went into serious decline in the Twenties. Its decline made low-rent factory space in the city increasingly available to the shoe industry and created unemployed workers who were willing to work at low wages. Capital outlay for shoe machinery was unnecessary; shoe shops in Lowell could lease machinery from the United Shoe Machinery Company of Beverly, Massachusetts. This leasing system allowed the shoe company great mobility in choosing its location or departing from a city when favorable conditions changed. Furthermore, the Massachusetts shoe industry had come under increasing competitive pressure in the Twenties from out-of-state manufacturers. This competition encouraged shoe shop owners to try to locate in areas where the cost of labor was low.

In the Twenties the shoe workers' unions in Massachusetts tried to handle this situation through state labor arbitration procedures, but under the impact of the Great Depression of the Thirties, manufacturers cut production and further lowered wages. Cuts in wages coupled with poor shop conditions encouraged the Shoe Workers' Protective Union, which had strong organizations in Newburyport, Haverhill, and Marlboro, to come to Lowell in 1933 to conduct a major strike.

The president of the Shoe Workers' Protective Union (SWPU), John Nolan, sent organizers into Lowell in early 1933. They reported unrest and dissatisfaction among the workers. It was still early enough in the shoe production season to allow preparations for a successful strike. Manufacturers' contracts would expire in June; their orders had to be filled by that date. Nolan first met with Mayor Charles Slowey, Chester Runels of the Lowell Chamber of Commerce, and Parker F. Murphy of the Lowell Trades and Labor Council to discuss the possibilities of avoiding a shoe strike. The city leaders did not respond satisfactorily to Nolan, and Charles Everett and Eugene DeBurro began to organize in Lowell for the SWPU.

The initial efforts of the SWPU were to protest against "sweat shop" conditions and to raise the wage scale in the shops. Yet the strike quickly evolved into a fight for union recognition and for the closed shop. It involved a struggle by the workers to control the means of production in order to stabilize an industry in which employment fluctuated according to style changes and production seasons.

Mayor Slowey recognized the potential damage of the strike, which began on April 7, and quickly attempted to resolve it. His first response was to appoint a committee made up of Attorney Joseph P. Donahue and Don L. Overlock, superintendent of the *Courier-Citizen* job plant. Donahue and Overlock were members of the rehabilitation committee of the Lowell Lodge of Elks, which had helped settle other labor disputes in the city. The mayor also created a citizens' committee made up of various clergymen and businessmen. His two committees failed to arrange a conference between the SWPU and the manufacturers, but they did meet with Nolan of the SWPU and individual groups of strikers.

The citizens' committee was, however, quickly abandoned by the mayor. He dismissed them on April 15, very early in the strike, with the explanation that the clergy could not afford to donate any more of their time because of the activities of Easter Week. However, the Reverend Appleton Grannis, Rector of St. Anne's Church and a member of the citizens' committee, protested that the citizens' committee had been promised changes in the poor working conditions at the shoe shops. The Fashion Wood Heel Company had been convicted in 1932 of violating state labor laws by employing minors. The District Court judge had continued the case for one year with the understanding that if the activity occurred again, he would pass sentence. A similar violation brought a $30.00 fine upon the Phyllis Shoe Company, which during the 1933 strike employed twenty-two minors, twenty hired as strikebreakers. United Novelty Shoe Company had sixteen violations of labor laws lodged against it in 1933 by the state labor department. Workers complained that one woman had received only 26 cents for a week's work, and that underpaid women employees had been hidden in a tunnel when the inspectors came around. Despite his concern for working conditions, Rev. Grannis urged a community settlement of the strike and rejected outside organizations such as the SWPU. The Elks committee admonished the strikers to return to work immediately and asked the manufacturers to grant an increase in wages. The committee urged the strikers to organize with a local union, not affiliated with SWPU, and settle disputes through the state arbitration board.

Mayor Slowey fretted publicly over the impact of the strike on the welfare rolls and on city taxes. An editorial in the *Lowell Courier-Citizen* on April 27, quoted the 1932 Chamber of Commerce records which described the shoe industry as employing 4,000 with a yearly payroll of $3 to $3.5 million. Local commercial banks handled that payroll. The shoe manufacturers occupied one million square feet of otherwise vacant mill space. The editor feared the economic hardships Lowell would undergo if such a payroll and the property taxes generated by the shoe industry were lost to the city.

Local labor organizations divided over support for the SWPU. Parker F. Murphy of the Lowell Trades and Labor Council favored the Boot & Shoe Workers' Union (AFL), the union with which the manufacturers preferred to deal. Murphy organized the leaders of the local Typographers' Union, the Stationary Firemen and Oilers' Union, and the Pressmen's Union in his efforts to pressure the shoe workers into acceptance of the manufacturers' position. On April 21 the SWPU asked the mayor to call upon the State Board of Conciliation and Arbitration to act. An invitation to the state board of arbitration to mediate the Lowell shoe strike came from Mayor Slowey on April 25, at the insistence of the United Leather Workers' Union local, an act which received the praise of Charles Everett, local organizer for the SWPU. The state board was composed of Attorney Edward Fisher of Lowell as chairman, John Campos of Fall River, the employees' representative, and Henry Wasgett of Newton, the employers' representative. However, the recent appointment of Edward Fisher as board chairman by the governor had caused vehement protest from the shoe workers' union in Brockton and from community groups across the state. Fisher was regarded by them as blatantly pro-manufacturer and oblivious to poor working conditions in industry.

The board's recommendations to settle the strike were basically the same as the Elks' committee. The strikers were to return to work immediately. Any grievances were to be settled locally or by the state board. But the state board also introduced the "Hudson Plan," an arbitration strategy in strike situations where a settlement between manufacturer and employees has been reached, but a closed shop, the requirements that all employees be union members, is the stumbling block. The closed shop is then traded off by the union in return for agreement on working conditions, wages, hours of labor, and the guarantee of shop stewards. In return, the manufacturer agrees not to lock out workers and to accept the union in his shop.

The shoe strikers' greatest weapons in 1933 were their solidarity, community support, and the use of intimidating violence against strikebreakers. The relief committee of the strikers obtained food, haircuts, and clothing from sympathetic groups in the community. In addition, about 800 workers of the United Leather Workers' Union, Local No. 2, met and endorsed the stand of the strikers, presenting the relief fund with a substantial check. They also publicly criticized the lack of support for the SWPU by the local Trades Council and Parker Murphy.

Unsympathetic press coverage, reports of other cities negotiating with the manufacturers to relocate, and the renewed threats by the manufacturers to re-locate their shops did not affect the strikers. Their relief organization on Central Street reported that 400 families, averaging six persons to a family, were being fed every day. Other efforts included fund-raising dances at the Commodore Ballroom and contributions from workers in other cities. In comparison with an alleged $7,000 slush fund raised by the manufacturers to combat the strike, these efforts to sustain 3,500 strikers seemed limited but adequate.

Throughout the course of the strike, frustration with strikebreakers led to sporadic acts of violence. Houses of workers who refused to go out on strike were bombarded by bricks on various occasions. An argument over the strike between two good friends resulted in the conviction of both on assault and battery charges. On April 26, Louis Arnois was treated at St. John's Hospital for a severe laceration of the scalp. It was reported that Arnois had been on Boston Road in Billerica with two companions checking on automobile registration numbers of cars bearing strikebreakers enroute to Lowell when the cars stopped and the assault took place.

Strike Breakers Quit City;
Escorted Through Angry Mob

Shoe Strike activity on Bridge Street, May 5, 1933 (Lowell Sun)

The use of police escorts for the cars of strikebreakers prompted reaction from the city council. Councillors Thomas Delaney and Thomas J. Markham asked the police superintendent to investigate the question of proper insurance coverage for automobiles serving to transport strikebreakers. Markham also contacted the chief inspector of the Registry of Motor Vehicles. Councillor Robert R. Thomas in a motion on May 2, 1933, commended the shoe strikers for their restraint and asked the superintendent of police to suspend the police escort and enforce all speed and traffic laws. After numerous complaints from Gorham Street residents about speeding violations by cars carrying strikebreakers, Councillor George W. O'Hare requested that the police drop their escort of the strikebreakers out of the city.

During the early stages of the strike, the manufacturers had refused to meet with organizers of the SWPU and maintained this position throughout the strike which last from April 7 to May 26. Gradually the strike picked up momentum with each side selecting its tactics. The strikers concentrated on the strikebreakers, and the manufacturers sought an injunction against picketing. Robert Becker, owner of Becker Brothers' Shoe Company, employed one-third of the workers who went out on strike. As spokesman for the manufacturers, Becker was the first to obtain an injunction against picketing. His plant was located on Bridge Street close to Memorial Auditorium. The strikers gathered regularly at the Auditorium to discuss the progress of the strike. As Becker began to bring strikebreakers from Boston, much of the strike agitation became concentrated at his plant. The manufacturers attempted to discredit the SWPU by offering a 10% wage increase, but only after the season's shoe contracts were filled. Once the peak production period was over, the bargaining power of the strikers would be destroyed. In a constant effort to weaken the strikers' position and to alarm the city, the shoe manufacturers announced to the press their intention to relocate.

Becker Brothers succeeded in obtaining temporary restraining orders against picketing from the Middlesex Superior Court. These restraining orders allowed only two pickets to patrol the entrances to the plants and prohibited interference with the employees and loitering or patrolling in the vicinity of the plants. This court action took the initiative from the strikers and protected the strikebreakers. The severe economic privation every worker must have felt in 1933 plus the continued daily transportation of out-of-town strike-

breakers aggravated the situation. The strikers responded with violence directed against Becker Brothers and their strikebreakers. On
May 5 according to the *Lowell Courier-Citizen*: "[t]he worst riot
this city has seen in recent years occurred in and about Kearney
Square late yesterday afternoon when striking shoe workers and
sympathizers clashed with loyal workers and strikebreakers."

The stress and the tension of the strike had grown into a major
confrontation. On May 4 minor trouble occurred outside of the
Becker Brothers' plant on Bridge Street when three men were arrested out of a group of several hundred strikers milling about the
plant. Early the next morning at the request of the strike committee,
Mayor Slowey addressed the strikers at the Memorial Auditorium.
The strikers had marched on City Hall on April 28, and they now
demanded that Slowey do something about the tension over the
strikebreakers. Slowey described himself as sympathetic with the
strikers and declared that if any strikebreakers possessed weapons
they would be prosecuted. He pleaded with the strikers to remain
peaceful but failed to convince them that he would act. That afternoon, as the strikebreakers left the Becker Brothers' plant, violence
erupted. The strikers halted them, sweeping aside the police. The
estimates of the number of strikers and sympathizers were as high
as 2,000. They began hurling objects at the vehicles that were waiting to take the strikebreakers out of Lowell. The incident on Bridge
Street lasted only twenty minutes, but the strikers and their sympathizers remained in the vicinity of Bridge Street, Kearney Square,
and Central Street until eight o'clock that night in the hope of
catching any strikebreakers who had not escaped. The *Courier-
Citizen* reported several scuffles between police and strikers, yet
many strikers actually prevented further violence by standing on
the running boards of the strikebreakers' automobiles, thereby
guaranteeing them safe conduct from the city and preventing what
might have been an ugly scene. Among them were individuals out
on bail from charges stemming from the disturbance the day before.

The mayor and Police Superintendent Hugh Downey had insisted that the police escort for the strikebreakers' cars was vital to
public safety. This policy continued to favor the shoe manufacturers against the strikers. Another incident occurred on May 9 when
a crowd of about three hundred strikers gathered in front of the
Alden Wood Heel Company on Warren Street to intercept about
fifty men and women employed by that firm. The *Lowell Sun* reacted
to the renewal of confrontation with great alarm:

> Though yesterday afternoon's demonstration was not as serious or
> spectacular as that of last Friday afternoon in Bridge Street, the
> demonstrators, from a police standpoint at least, were far more hostile
> than they encountered to date in demonstrations locally. Police were
> utterly powerless in attempts to handle the vast throng until tear gas
> bombs were brought into use.

Becker Brothers and the Alden Wood Heel Company later brought
contempt charges against the strikers. The impasse in the strike
negotiations and the times of stress and idleness made the strikebreaker the focal point for frustration and violence. However, the
open confrontation between strikers and police threatened to erode
community sympathy. An editorial from the *Lowell Sunday Telegram*
of May 9 declared:

> Whether it be due to a decadence in the standard of our industrial
> population, whether it can be attributed to "Red" influence or to
> something else, there has been a campaign of violence and intimida-
> tion of late that does not square with Lowell's past reputation as an
> industrial city.

However, a more temperate editorial in the *Courier-Citizen* pointed
out:

> We have been rather sympathetic with the strikers. They had some
> points where they scored against the employers. . . . The brick throw-
> ing and rioting, however, cool off enthusiasm for the cause. We don't
> care for strikebreakers, either. They invite trouble . . . [violence]
> doesn't help. It hurts. . . . The cooler heads among the strikers ought
> to insist on methods that will get results.

Reacting to the week of violence in the streets of Lowell, Mayor
Slowey appealed to Democratic Governor Joseph B. Ely to intervene. Over the course of three days from May 10 to May 12, the
governor met in Boston with Mayor Slowey, City Solicitor James H.
Gilbride, Attorney Frederick W. Mansfield of Boston, counsel for
the strikers, Nolan of the SWPU, Fisher, the chairman of the state
arbitration board, and the manufacturers and their lawyers. Although no details of the conference were reported, the governor apparently did his utmost for a speedy settlement. In an address to the
strikers on May 25, Nolan stated that the governor had stood
behind them despite tremendous pressures on him to call in state
police or the state militia.

After seven weeks of stalemated negotiation, a settlement was
reached. A vote by the strikers was taken on May 26 in the Memorial Auditorium, where the crowd was reported at 3,000. A total of

1,350 votes were cast, 708 in favor of the settlement, 595 opposed, and 47 were blank. The large number of negative votes objected to the lack of a closed shop provision in the settlement. The major provisions were recognition of the SWPU but no closed shop. Non-union workers would continue to find jobs in Lowell shoe shops. An immediate 10% wage increase was granted, effective no later than August 1, as well as non-discrimination in rehiring strikers, the creation of shop stewards to represent the workers, preference of Lowell labor in all new hiring, work during slack periods to be divided equally among the regular crew, and the establishment of the 48 hour work week. All four contempt cases against the strikers were dropped as part of the settlement. At the meeting, Nolan, Leo Hamilton, general secretary of the SWPU, and the union's attorney, Mansfield, all stressed the disunity among the strikers over violence against strikebreakers and the exhaustion of the negotiation process. The closed shop remained the touchy issue, but the influence of Robert Dempsey, Vice-President of the local SWPU, who was well liked by the strikers, was decisive. Dempsey said he was 100% behind the strikers on the closed shop, but that he was convinced there was no recourse at present but to accept the agreement as it stood. It was, however, a limited victory in the eyes of many.

The settlement split the solidarity of the Lowell shoe manufacturing companies. The Lowell Shoe Company, United Novelty, Merrimack, Majestic, John C. Pilling Shoe Companies, the Fashion Wood Heel, and the Alden Wood Heel Company signed the agreement. C.V. Watson Shoe Company relocated in Auburn, Maine. Becker Brothers' Shoe Company, which had led the manufacturers' opposition, also left Lowell. The Laganas and the Foster Shoe Companies continued to negotiate with the union and contemplate relocation.

The shoe strike in Lowell stimulated additional worker militancy in the area in 1933. Strikes occurred at the Fletcher Quarry in North Chelmsford and at the Lowell Fertilizer Company, the latter resulting in a 25% wage increase. Wage increases of 10% or more were granted to the American Hide and Leather employees, to workers at the American Woolen Company, Lowell Uxbridge Worsted Company, and others. Labor activity sparked by the shoe workers obtained some relief from the downward spiral of wages in the early Thirties.

In summation, the striking shoe workers increased their wages, obtained recognition, and won the means to alleviate sweat shop

working conditions through shop stewards and grievance procedures and to improve labor conditions in general. The strikers
forced these agreements through organization and militancy. However, the closed shop, the strongest protection for union workers,
was denied them. The political influence of the governor, the
mayor, and the city council emphasized the urgency of a settlement
with little regard for the objectives of the strikers, but the strike had
resulted in the organization of Lowell shoe workers in 1933 and
forced the manufacturers to be thereafter more responsive to their
interests.

YVONNE HOAR:
MILL WORKER, UNION ORGANIZER,
SHOP STEWARD

Lewis T. Karabatsos

I was born in North Adams, Massachusetts, December 27, 1908. We moved from there, and I don't remember North Adams 'cause I was only a year old when we left there. We moved to Clinton, and I started school in Clinton. I was only there a few months when we moved to Lowell. My father worked in the mills in North Adams and his boss moved to Lowell, so he asked him to come with him and that's why he came to Lowell then. My father was a machinist. He always worked in the Merrimack Mills for forty years. He worked on all kinds of machinery, any type of machine that broke down. They had treadles, they had the weave room, they had the dye works, and in the finishing room they had the peg machines. They used to have the velvet running through them. They had all kinds of machines they had to fix in there. In later years he'd assemble them. Instead of running one machine they added two machines together. A little later when they saw that went good, well, they added three machines. That took the work of three girls; one girl could run the three whole machines. And they had the brush machines where they could brush the velvet. All kinds of machines like that. He'd done all the repairing on them.

When he first came to Lowell he was getting twenty-five cents an hour, that was his wages then. The wages were not too, too good. But he worked day and night. He used to work, I remember when

we were kids. For seven years he never wore a white collar. He
wore dark shirts, these dark grey shirts. Oh, like the iceman used to
wear then. Just laborers used to wear them, just the dark clothes,
the dark grey shirts. Nothing fancy, because he'd be all grease, and,
of course, when he got into them he'd wear overalls over them.
He'd go to the early mass on Sunday and go right to work and
come back home at six or seven o'clock. He worked every Sunday
of his life. He'd have to go back to work, then he'd work 'till ten or
twelve o'clock at night in the mill. And I remember the year my
brother Raymond was born. He came home, and he'd brought his
pay. He'd made a hundred dollars. That was clear, of course, there
was no income tax in them days. He had a hundred dollars, and
that was a great thing. He thought that was the biggest money.
They never thought they'd see a hundred dollars in their hands
and that was the biggest pay he'd ever made.

When we first came to Lowell, we moved to Prince Street, and
there were corporation houses there. They were dismal and dreary-
looking. My mother was petrified; she wouldn't leave us out of the
house. So we stayed there for about three days 'till they found a
place on Salem Street. Then we moved up over Barrett's store. Barrett had a grocery store, a meat market on Salem Street, right on the
corner of Salem and Decatur Street. Ross Paper Shop was on one
corner and Barrett's was right across the street. Today I guess it's
the housing projects that are in there now. The corporation houses
on Prince Street were dark. You'd have to have lights on all day
'cause you couldn't see. It was all lamps in them days; they had
them everywhere, including Salem Street. But that was a bright
tenement. The stairs were over the store and it was bright; it wasn't
all closed in. On Prince Street we were all in one length. It'd run
from one street light to a back alley in the back of the house. The
rooms were one right after another like stalls in fact, and it was all
lamps, gas jets they had there, they mostly used lamps. I was doing
my homework one night, taking care of my kid sister. We were
living on Salem Street, and she was only a baby then. We were sitting. I was sitting around the side of the table where the lamp was
and the first thing, I turned around and she had her both hands on
the chimney, the lamp chimney, and she burned the inside of her
hands, both from the lamp chimney. I was petrified, but the poor
kid screamed. She felt the pain and that was the only time I noticed
it. We didn't know any better then. Oh, there were plenty of incidents, fires and all. Knocking over kerosene lamps, they were
dangerous, but they were all used then.

I started school in Clinton. Just started three months then we came to Lowell, where we went to St. Joseph's school on Moody Street. That was a French school then. Of course, in Clinton you couldn't speak French; they were all English-speaking people. We had this old lady boarder. This lady boarded with us, this Miss Green from North Adams to Clinton to Lowell. She stayed with us all of her life. She was an old maid, had nobody, so she stayed with us. And we couldn't speak French but my mother enrolled us in school she said that we were French. Then we got into school the teacher sent for my mother. She said "I thought you were French. How come the children can't speak French?" My mother said, "Well we are, but they can't speak it 'cause they were all brought up as English-speaking people." We never learned French, we knew a few words, and that's when we first started learning French, in St. Joseph's.

And from there we moved to Cumberland Road. They bought a house finally. They found this place over in Centralville, and they bought that house. There was almost every nationality. There was Irish and French and Greek people. There were different nationalities in Centralville, it was a mixture. I went to St. Louis' School then, and stayed there in St. Louis' School until I graduated from grammar school. And I never went to high school or anythin' else 'cause I got a job then. Just before graduation I took this job minding five kids, five dollars a week. It was just a couple of streets up from us so I thought that was wonderful. I just wanted to get to work and make some money. I took the job and I've been working ever since. The people I worked for were French. He was a painter, and she worked in a mill. I don't know what mill. I think it was the Massachusetts that she worked in at the time, and she had five small children. I took care of the five small kids for about a year or so. From then my sister got a job in the hospital in Boston, in St. Elizabeth's Hospital. I was only fifteen then, so I could go but I had to go to school an afternoon a week. We had to go to vocational school a half day a week because we weren't of age. So I left in 1923 and went down to Boston and worked there with her for a year in the hospital cafeteria.

[The interviewer asks if the reason she went to work at fifteen was her family's economic need.] No, no, no, it wasn't, because my father worked all the time. We weren't rich, and we weren't poor. We never wanted for anything, but we never had any luxuries, that's for sure. Just the necessities, three squares a day, and my mother was a very handy person. She made all our clothes, and she

done all the sewing for all of us. She used to go to Pollard's Basement. Pollard's was a very big store then, and they used to have a
lot of bargains. They'd buy stockings that'd go up to here from all
the different hosieries, and they'd pick them over and they sold
them for a penny a piece. Then she'd pick them over, then she'd
take them home and sew them, try to match them as best she could
and sew them together. Then when you wore your long johns in
the winter with those black stockings over them you'd be bow-
legged, lumpy — what a mess! That used to irritate me more than
anything in my life. I used to cry every time I put them on in the
morning. In fact we all did.

I worked at the hospital for a year. And that was right after I had
my appendix out, so I went home in 1924 and went into the mill. I
worked at the Merrimack. I went into the weave room where they
were gonna teach me; in them days they called it the "battery
girls." They had big wide machines, and they had great big reels at
the end of it, and they put the bobbins in there. And you'd thread it
on the side. But they don't call them "battery girls" no more. In the
Wannalancit Mill they were "unifil girls." Later on when I went
into Wannalancit, they asked me what I used to do and I said, "Oh,
I was a battery girl," and they looked at me and laughed. I said,
"What are they called?" and he said, "They're unifil girls," and I
said, "So what?" I only stayed one day in the weave room. It was
the noisiest room you could ever be in. There's machines going and
shuttles going back and forth, and sometimes they'd fly off, and
they were pointed things and if they ever hit you, boy, you'd know
it. Those flying shuttles, they're dangerous. In fact, mother got
struck by one in the leg. Then the thing in between [the harness of
the loom] with all the wires hanging off, it pushes the thread up
and the thread goes in and pushes it back, and it [the reed] keeps
plopping back and forth. It's very, very noisy. In fact, the whole
place vibrates. When I come out of there at night I was shaking; I
was still in the mill. It's a place you have to get used to; it's the noisiest place in the whole mill in fact. Then I told my father I didn't
like it, and he said, "well, you weren't getting paid for it anyways,
you were just in there to learn to see if you liked it. I didn't get paid
for the whole day's work, they were just teaching me.

So then they put me up in the finishing room where I worked for
Peter Burroughs. He was an old man then, and he had both of his
legs cut off. He had sugar diabetes, and they had cut both of his legs
off and he was in a wheelchair, but he was still the boss there. And
that's where those machines were, one by one. Then they started

putting two together, then three together. They were doubling up all the machines so it made that much more work and less help to go by. In the finishing room I used to run these silent pegs, they called them. They'd put a load of velvet which was all cut by then, in the back and a big iron wheel would run through the pegs. They had these great big reels that used to run the velvet through them. You'd have to thread the cloth in through the back; they'd go through these pegs and be hit by another piece of iron. With one machine, sometimes you'd have to run them two or three times, but with the three machines together I'd only have to do it once. It saved a lot of time. Sometimes it'd have to go through six times, then it'd go to a brush machine, then to a folder. I'd run them folders, all you'd do is sit back and let it fold back and forth. There we got thirteen dollars a week. No matter who you are or where you were in the mill, you got thirteen dollars a week. You might as well have taken a deck of cards and passed it out. You really didn't need names, 'cause everyone got thirteen dollars a week. The one with the easiest job and with the hardest job got the same money as the rest of them. Wouldn't do you any good to complain; they'd never complain. They were so petrified for their jobs in them days, it was pitiful.

If you were a good worker, in with the boss, it was O.K., you weren't scared. But the others, the least little thing and those snoopers would snoop on you and would tell the boss and you'd be out. They talk about patronage these days; there was nothing like it in the mill. That's what finally drove the Merrimack out of business, it had too much patronage. Neither color, creed or nationality, or anything else. Your creed; if you were a Catholic you didn't fit worth a darn; 'cause I remember Fox [the superintendent at the Merrimack] saying that a Catholic would never work in the office of the Merrimack. So therefore, in the long run, year by year, people started getting a little smarter and started talking about forming a union. Louis Vergados is the one who started the union in the Merrimack. He sent out this pamphlet that said to come to a meeting 'cause we were going to start a union. It was 1938. They were passing out the pamphlets. I still have one, I had my name in one of them because I was one of the agitators. My son should keep this. They were going to have this meeting, and they all kept talking about it. All the girls kept saying, are you going, are you going, and I said, "Of course not." I asked my girlfriend, "Are you going to go?" She said, "I'll go if you go," and I said, "You won't go,'cause you're chicken." She said, "Alright we're going, we're going right after work tonight." And we went, and that's where I got implicated

by shooting my big mouth off. Telling them all different things.
How the bosses were unfair to the help, which they were, and how
there was one clique which could do anything they wanted, and it
didn't matter. Let the other poor fools do anything, they'd be
bounced right out. And if anyone died in your immediate family,
they'd take up a collection.

Thank God, no one in my family did but I had friends, one close
friend whose mother died. It was on Mother's Day, and I started to
pick up a collection but nobody could be bothered. Then one of the
girls in the clique, Alice, well, she had a sister down in Florida and
her husband died. Immediately they started taking up a collection,
and everybody had to give for poor Alice's sister's husband! Well
that's when I blew my stack. I told Louis all about it. And he said,
"Why don't you come on the committee?" and I said, "No, I couldn't
do that," but they persuaded me and I ended up becoming a shop
steward. I didn't set out to become mill steward.

But if you don't think I didn't catch it then. Well, they were going
to throw me in the canal and everything else. Well, the boss started
getting real cocky. At night we went to ring out our cards, and
there was a little clique going out ahead of time, so they'd run and
punch their cards first. And they'd walk out. If any of us did it, the
boss would come down and say, "Get back to work until five of,"
and no one would ever say it was after five of or they'd get
bounced. They tried to bounce me a couple of times, but my father
had worked there for so long and he was the one who had gotten
me the job. I remember one day Peter Burroughs came by [in his
wheelchair] and piled a whole load of velvet in back of me. Well, I
didn't have any work, and I was waiting for the boys to come and
bring me some. So he comes around and says, "Why didn't you do
that work in the back?" and I said, "Cause it wasn't there!" and he
said, "You liar, it was so there!" Well, I was a cocky little bugger
then, and I jumped up and said, "Don't call me a liar. You just now
put that there, and I'm sitting here watching you do it. Don't you
dare call me a liar or I'll bat you on the side of the head! You dirty
Englishman!" He took off, and I hollered, not so loud anymore,
after him, "And you know what you can do with your job!" Well, I
walked down to the dressing room, it was a room with hooks in it
where the girls used to hang their coats, and there was a curtain
across the front of it. The men had one on the other side. So I put on
my hat and coat. I knew I was going to get killed by my father when
I got home. First of all for jacking up. I was going out the door, and
he [Burroughs] said, "Don't be so hasty, don't be so hasty, get back

to work." "No, I won't," I said. Just then my father comes walking through, and he says, "Joe, where'd you get that spitfire? She has more darn nerve than anybody." "He just called me a liar and I'm not a liar," I said. My father said, "Get back to work, get back to work." I said, "I'm not going back to work for him." I had to get back to work because my father told me to. Then Burroughs says, "You started it, you started it," so he comes in and starts to push things here and there. He wanted to get in good with me then. Anyways there were these windows in the Merrimack that were close to the door and opened out. He says, "Push me down the room," and I said, "I'll push you down the room, I have a good mind to push you out the window!" "Get out of here, get out of here. leave me alone!" he said. He never asked me to push him again.

Let's see, after that I worked in the clothroom. That was a better job. But there was more patronage in there than in the other place. And they favored people of English background, and your bosses and supers and higher-ups were English. And if you were anything else, they looked at you like you were dirt. You were dirt that's all, and I was still getting the thirteen dollars a week. At that time there wasn't much work in the finishing room and rather than lay me off, because of my father — not because I was a good worker, because they didn't like me that much — they put me in the clothroom. And I stayed there a few years. I got married while I was in the finishing room, then moved up to the clothroom. That's where we started the union in the clothroom. That's when my father disowned me. He said, "I never thought I'd see my daughter standing at the gate, talking to a union leader." He almost killed me. But he wouldn't join. He had been there too long, and I told him he was afraid for his job. But they got him out anyways; he was getting older, and they were replacing everybody with younger men.

As steward in the union, I had to take their complaints, and everyone had complaints. The least little thing, of course. It was a new union, and we had never been in a union before. Well, this guy from the State Labor Board in Boston came down. He wanted to ask some of the girls questions, one by one in the office. I guess it was alright, but I said, "No, you don't, I'm gonna be in there too." He said, "No, you aren't, this isn't any of your business. I'm head of the Labor Board, and this has nothing to do with your union." So I stayed out, and I called Louis. I said, "He's in there questioning all the girls, and he won't let me in." He laughed and said, "That's O.K. Yvonne, you'll meet him after work; come up because we're going to have a meeting up here." And he was there. He said, "So, this is the little one who wanted to come in." And I said, "Yes, but you wouldn't let me." He said, "Listen, Yvonne, learn to crawl before you learn to walk."

Then things started to get so bad that McKay had to hire a personnel manager. They couldn't control him. Well, Whittier was my boss then, Rigby had died and Whittier was made boss. And they were going in the clique again, running to punch their cards, and he came down one night and I was first at the clock. He says, "It's not five of yet, Yvonne," and I says, "Yes, it is, the green light's on." "You're not supposed to have your hat and coat on yet," and I said, "That's because I'm a little faster than them, so I have them on." He says, "You're supposed to be at your bench." "Wait a minute, Whittier," I says, "Whenever anyone else is in line, it's all stiff and grins. They can punch anytime they want to. Nobody says anything to them. You don't say anything to them." I was shop steward at the time. "Just because we do it, the others do it. You're not going to make flesh of one and fish of another, the way this place has been run all their lives. Well, you're not going to do it no more."

So the help got cocky, we all got cocky. In fact they're not going to push it down our throats like before. They got their rights. They know what they could do and what they couldn't do. They weren't going to infringe on their rights. They'd come over, "Hey Yvonne, look what they're trying to make me do." And boy, the fellas, they were the worst. They'd push me on. They agitated me more than anybody. They'd come down and say, "Hey, they done this to me." So of course, I'd have to go into the office and squawk. We talked it over, and then the floor lady, Mrs. Camp, she was English too. She was a snip if there ever was one. And she was always trying to rub it in to one girl or the other, so finally I got her in the office one day, with Bell, he was the super then, and he starts talking about what the girls were doing. And I says, "It's no more than right, the other girls are doing it, Mr. Bell, why can't she do it?" And she says, "Well Yvonne, you're a pretty good talker, but," she says, "things aren't right. They haven't been right since the union started." I says, "If it wasn't for you, and people like you and the likes of you, there never would have been a union in this place. But it was the likes of you that brought the unions in," I says, "If there wasn't so much partiality for one to another," I says, "and that's the whole thing in a nutshell." One day, I don't know what it was over, they all went on strike, the whole mill. So they had to go get the personnel manager. They went and got the personnel, and he says, "I'm firing your leader," meaning me. And they said, "You're

gonna what?" and they all rushed him. I was petrified; I thought
sure to God they were gonna kill him. They all raced to the door
after him. Boy, did he go running! He ran out of that room so fast,
and then, of course, the whole kit and caboodle stopped.

And of course, they all got their raises even the ones that didn't
want to join the union. Louis said, "Talk 'em into it or fire them."
"No, Louis," I says, "I'm not going to talk 'em into it. If they don't
want to join, they don't want to join. This isn't a closed shop or
anything. They're not bothering anybody," I says, "Leave 'em
alone." He says, "Jesus, those broads!" I says, "They're not broads,
Louis, they're girls, they're young ladies." He says, "Since when;
they're old maids." "Nonetheless," I says, "They're girls who have
been here a good many years, and I'm not having them lose their
jobs over the union," I says, "I admit if they weren't doing their
work or something, but we got things we want now, we've got our
rights now and everything else. So let it stand at that." That's the
way it stood for quite a while. But we were all discriminating then
because there was a war going on. I says, "What are you talking
about, there's a war going on, you're young men, what are you
doing here, you're old enough to go in. I got a brother who's in the
service; I got friends who are in the service. They're fighting for
this war. I don't see you people doing too much of anything for it."
So that's alright, I insulted them. So we had a meeting about it in
the office.

Our union dues weren't very high, about a quarter a month, and
the benefits were better working conditions, you weren't getting
fired, you weren't afraid of turning your head and getting fired for
it, you could speak up about lies, certain ones would go in the main
office and everything and lie about the help, and some poor soul
would get bounced for no reason at all. With the union, they could
go in and fight for their cause. So they'd go and fight, and we
fought plenty. But it got so bad that after a while they didn't want
to give in to the union; they didn't want the help to run the place
either. So they got the personnel agent in there, when Fox left, they
had this Lewis as personnel agent. Finally it went from bad to
worse, and the mill went down and they sold out. Ziskind bought
the whole place. They'd be putting in overtime for men, and they
weren't even there. When they got paid, they'd have to split it up
with the bosses, and when they finally caught up with them [the
supervisors], they called it the Teapot Dome thing. A whole bunch
of them got fired because of it. It was bigger than the Teapot Dome
thing. Even in the beginning, they'd bring help in from Canada

and, the poor souls, the bosses would take part of their pay for getting them jobs. They'd take so much of their pay every week for a
certain length of time. If they bought furniture or anything, I saw
your furniture men in Lowell get rich; they'd sell them furniture.
They'd repossess it if the poor souls lost their jobs. They'd take back
the furniture and make them buy it back from them again.

They hired all sorts of cheap labor: Greeks, Italians, French. Not
the English. All the English got the good jobs. All us foreigners got
the poor jobs. But I got my end in anyways when I went in the
office there, when I was on the committee with Louis Vergados.
Fox was telling us how good he was to us, how he done this for us
and how he hadn't done this and hadn't done that for us. So I said
to him, "You yourself said there'd never be a Catholic working in
the office. Is there a Catholic working in the office?" He said, "Well,
there must be." I said, "There ain't a damn one in there and you
know it. There ain't one Catholic in that whole office, not in the
main office, the mill office, or anywhere else." They were all Protestant, not that they weren't nice girls, they were lovely girls. But just
to show you how narrow-minded and black-hearted they were --
very, very, narrow-minded. And the poor Greek fellows that
worked in the dye house. No wonder "Sampascoopies" -- did you
ever read his column [in the *Lowell Sun*] "Sampascoopies?" -- he
said, "No wonder the people of Lowell died of consumption and
everything else in the mills." And he was referring to the Merrimack Mills specifically, he said once in the paper. The poor fellas
would come in wearing only pants and drawers in the vats there.
They'd go in and their arms would be bare because they'd have to
drag the cloth out of the vats. Their stomachs would be blue, green,
purple, whatever the color happened to be at that time. It was hot,
they'd sweat. It was wicked. You wouldn't put a human being to
work in a place like that. They were afraid for their jobs. They were
meek. They were browbeaten. There was so little around, although
you heard a little of wealth, they were too proud. They'd work for
their money at no matter how degrading a job rather than go on
welfare. There was very little welfare then. You very seldom heard
of it.

Sometimes there was trouble between the French and the Irish.
The Irish were instigators. They were up across the common, the
North Common. If you went up on the Common, they had swings
and teeters and all that. There's always be a fight between the
French and the Irish. The Irish would come up, "Are you French?"
They'd knock the stuffings out of ya. And the Greek kids would be

recognized because they'd go to the Greek schools, and they'd wear sort of a blue pinafore uniform. That's how you could distinguish them from other nationalities; so they got hell kicked out of them too by the Irish. But don't worry, the Irish got theirs too. On Saturdays when they'd come down to Hart's Bakery for their beans, many a beanpot was spilled and broken for the wallops we took during the week. You don't see any more of that. That went out gradually as we started growing older and getting jobs and such. There was some of that after, but that was from the younger kids. I don't know why all this happened. I just don't know. We may have been in a minority group then I think. The English must have carted over all the Irish people. They developed the canals. They are the ones that opened the canals and all. There were more Irish than us. We were scattered all over the place. Then the Greeks started building up. Then Market Street and Salem Street were right close together.

*   *   *   *

I got married in 1927. We first moved to Erie Street. That was my first home up on Erie Street. It was a nice little place too. It was very nice, quiet and much too big for us. We had a living room and a dining room, the kitchen and the bedroom, and there's two other rooms beside and a washroom. We had steam heat. I bought a gas stove. No brains, you know, when you first get married, you think you're going to live there the rest of your life. So that was alright. I moved from there to Dalton Street. That was a nice tenement; we lived there for a few years. A nice old lady lived downstairs from us. We paid seven dollars a week down on Erie Street, and I think we paid the same on Dalton Street; that was a good rent for that time. Then we moved to Lawrence where my husband worked for Best Goods. No, it was Portsmouth, New Hampshire, I take that back. From Portsmouth we moved to Lawrence. From Lawrence we moved back to Lowell. I stayed home for three years, and the boy was three years old when I decided I was going back to work. The Depression was starting, and things were getting pretty slack. There was no work or anything. So I went back to work in the famous cloth works all over again. That was before all this looney stuff started again. The baby was three years old then; he worked, and I worked. He'd take the baby up to his mother's and I'd go to work, then at night I'd get out of work and go to his mother's and pick him up. I didn't find that too hard at the time. But later he started getting older, and he was starting to get rambunctious. Grammy was having a hard time chasing after him. So, there was a day nursery [the Lowell Day Nursery on Cabot Street] the same place it is today, in the corporation. And I went in one day and found out how they went about it. How you brought the children in and how much it cost. She said she'd be glad to have George, and that it was a nice place with a yard with swings and teeters and everything. I gave him a breakfast, and they had a light lunch in the morning. At noon they had their dinner, then they had a light lunch in the afternoon. It cost seventy-five cents a week; they'd take care of him. So then in the morning it was the problem of getting George across the bridge. We lived in the block at the corner, and we'd have to walk across the Aiken Street Bridge. That was an operation but it wasn't too bad, and then at night I'd pick him up on my way home. It was on my way home, of course, my husband would be working later. I didn't mind that at all, but I found the Depression hard to get through. It was nip and tuck all the time. Of course, things were cheap, dirt cheap, but your money was so small. We were fortunate because he got a job with the W.P.A., and I still had my job in the Merrimack. But I was only getting nine dollars a week then. But out of the goodness of his heart, Whittier kept me. I was a good worker. He knew that I was married and that I had a baby then. My husband was out of work for a while, then he got on W.P.A. and I was working in the mill. We were fortunate then, compared to some poor souls. There was some pretty bad off, and there were bread lines all over the place.

The poor souls had nothing. They'd rob Peter to pay Paul, and brazen we were. He had friends in business, we were brazen then. We'd bought a radio during the Depression and paid a dollar a week for it. Every week I'd give him a dollar, and he'd go down and pay on it. One day he was going down, and he saw this friend, and he said, "Where are you going?" and he says, "I'm going down to pay on my radio. I owe two weeks on it." His friend says, "Give the two dollars to me. I'll give it to you in a couple of days, as soon as business comes in." He says, "Gee, I gotta pay on it," and he says, "I'll give it to you in a couple of days when I get the money." So he gives him the money. Then he got the two dollars in his business. He was a good guy, and he gave it back. They all helped one another and like that. People were very good to one another in them days. They shared a lot. If you didn't have something and they did, they'd give it to you. If you had neighbors and you didn't have anything to eat, they'd take you in and feed you. If they didn't have anything, well you fed them. They'd feed you, and you'd feed them. That's the way it was then. They were all pretty good in them days, but today I don't know.

Rear of Workers' housing, Little Canada, 1930s (Library of Congress)

In the Thirties we had a hurricane and we had a flood, and the 1936 flood was bad. Two floods — I only count the one that come up to my window. It come right up to the first floor window right on the corner of Aiken Street and Lakeview Avenue. There was a drugstore right there on the corner, and it came right up to the windows. And it went all the way up to Dalton Street, the corner of Dalton and Aiken and Ludlam, that's as far as it went. They had fishermen from Gloucester in boats, taking them out. And we were there — we had stayed overnight. Anyways, the Red Cross came around and was evacuating everybody, but we had fallen fast asleep and hadn't heard anybody. Then at five in the morning we looked out the window, and we were the only ones on the block. Only us three and the guy downstairs. But further down the street on the Aiken Street side, there was an old woman, and she was alone too. They evacuated her too. Well, we had to go up over the roof and came down the Aiken Street side. We climbed through the second floor window into a boat. It was a Gloucester fisherman that came, and there was one fellow there who had only a hook, he didn't have a hand there. He was a powerful young fella too. I remember because he lifted us all into the boat. The old lady there, he lifted her in and she was petrified. She had a pocketbook with her, and she must have had all her worldly goods in it. She hung onto it. I told her, "Give me you pocketbook until you get into the boat," and she said, "No, no, no," and she wouldn't let go of it either. She give me the dirtiest look. Finally we all got in. Of course, they tried to balance the boat so they put Buddy [Yvonne's son] in the back of the boat with the other fellas and me up there in front. When the boat started, it scared the kid and me, he almost jumped in the water. And George said, "It's alright, he's just scared is all," and we rode up to the firehouse. It looked like coming in from the old country, everybody standing up there waiting for all the refugees to come in. There was too much water there, so the guy picked us up in his arms and carried us over to dry land. Everyone would stand up and holler and cheer. It was so foolish! Bunch of nuts! So that's alright. So I went and stayed with my mother until the water receded and then when it did, nothing. Wasn't any bridges. The bridge had collapsed. So they built stairs, like rope stairs with rope handles. You had to go all the way down on one side and climb all the way back up on the other. I was petrified to go down them and up. But you got used to it until they repaired the bridge. They didn't repair the bridge for quite a while. Everything was washed out. There was a little house down the street, in back of the club. It got washed down the Merrimack. Here one minute, gone the next. We had to get all brand new furniture. Barns came down, cows, horses, chicken coops with chickens in them. It was unbelievable. If anyone had ever told me, I never would have believed them. No, I never would have believed them. I was sitting in the window watching them float by. Everything, animals, furniture, just float by. Oh, and we were starving then for God's sakes. There wasn't too much around. We lived four flights up, really out of the reach of the water. But what if there had been a fire? We never thought of that. If there had been a fire, we all would have been gone. We wouldn't have had a chance.

*   *   *   *

During World War II I left the Merrimack Mills and went to the Remington for two years. They were making bullets and everything for the war. Gee, I got good money there. A dollar and a quarter or a dollar and a half an hour. I think I got a dollar seventy-five. That was good money then. I inspected bullets. They'd have big conveyors. They'd have the conveyors in front of you and a big case of bullets. You'd inspect them and then put so many in a box and put them on a conveyor. It was a good little job. You'd have to work change-shifts, night and days. The middle shift would appreciate the change. That was the hardest part of it. Getting used to that. But outside of that it was a pretty good little job. Once I left the Merrimack, I was done with the union. I wasn't as cocky then. I was calming down. They were paying better money at the Remington, and the Merrimack wasn't doing so hot then. It was starting to go down. They weren't doing too, too good. Most all mills weren't doing too good then. Because they didn't have the help. They were all flocking to Remington for the better money. After I left there, I stayed home for quite a while until one of his [her husband's] sisters got into an automobile accident, and she died. The other sister was left alone, and she was sick. She was alone so that's why we came here, to stay with her. So we came and stayed here a year and a half. I was at the Wannalancit then, and I had learned spooling. For all the years I had been in a mill I hadn't learned spooling. I had seen it done. Oh, I was in another mill too, on Jackson Street. I was only a kid then and had to go to vocational school one afternoon a week. And I was making good money there. I was making sixty-nine cents an hour. That was good money then, considering what they paid in other mills. I was doing something called doffing. After the yarn was all wound on spools, I'd take it off and they'd weigh it. Then they'd get as much yarn as would be twirled all around the spool. Spooling is similar to that. So I started spooling. That's why, when I went into the Wannalancit, they asked, "What did you do in the mill?" and I says, "I was a battery girl." He says, "You're dating yourself, Yvonne. Battery girls went out a long time ago!" But I had been out of the mill a long time. I went to the shoe shops. That's where I went, to the shoe shops. I worked in a few shoe shops then. I did almost everything! I'd put the polish on them. Then from dressing, I went to packing, and from packing I went to floor girl. Floor girl -- you'd have to pick up the shoes, you know, the defects, and you'd take them down to get repaired, where they'd have them repaired. If it was a heel, you'd take it to the heeler; if it was the vamp, you'd bring it over to the vamper, anything like that. Then you'd take it to the repair girls. They'd grain it over, then they'd bring it back and I'd have to pack them. The floor girl -- I'd have to take all the shoes the girls had made, take them back, and pack them in their cases. I'd watch their numbers. They go by numbers for the sizes and pack them away. That was a good little job too. You couldn't stop for a minute though, without somebody yelling, "I need this, I need that." That was alright though. It was after I left, I quit there, that I went to Wannalancit, I liked it there. I was spooling, and I was working nights which I had never done except when I worked at Remington. So I could sleep in the morning. I always got up at 5:30 in the morning, and I always said I'm going to get a job where I can sleep in the morning. So I started one to nine. So that was good because it was only he and I. He worked in the afternoon. No, he was retired then. He'd drive me to work and pick me up. I liked that, I could have gone on there forever. But I came here when I retired. I was sixty-two then, and that was three years ago. So I retired then. That's the only job I miss out of all of them, the Wannalancit. I can't go back because I can't go back to the same job I left, that I was working at. That's one of the conditions about working "on the railroad," that you can't go back to the job that you left. I can't see where that's got anything to do with working on the railroad; I can see where it might be to keep him from working on another railroad. But the women get pensions too, just like the men. He gets a pension, and I also get a pension and I get my social security pension, but I can't go back at the last job that I left. So I can't go back to the same place.

JAMES ELLIS:
MILL WORKER, BUSINESS AGENT, CIO ORGANIZER

by Karen Ahlin

In 1938 at the age of nineteen, I was working in the dye house at the Merrimack Manufacturing Company in Lowell. The dye house is what is commonly known as the color room where the cloth is dyed after it is woven and finished upstairs. I had a partner working next to me, and we used to start work at seven in the morning. From seven 'till nine in the morning, you couldn't see one or two feet beyond you because of the steam that was generated as you started work. And that steam would sort of fade away around nine or ten o'clock. One morning as the steam evaporated, I looked for my partner, and he was lying on the floor from a heart attack. The man had seven children, and was sixty-five years old. At that time we were earning $13.40 a week for a forty hour week. I went to his assistance, and my boss immediately came forward and instructed me to get back to my machine. He would not let me administer first aid to a man who was at that moment dying. It was at least a half an hour before the nurse came down with the doctor who then declared the man dead. From that moment on, I'd made up my mind that the only way that we workers could elevate our standard of living was to organize collectively into a union.

Unions were few and far between. The plant that we worked for, the Merrimack Manufacturing Company, employed about 3,000 people. I immediately set out to organize, not knowing anything

Dye house worker mixing colors (Merrimack Valley
Textile Museum)

House, to the State Board of Mediation and the Labor Relations
Board. I presented them with the cards. A meeting was called between the company and the union we had formed. In the mean-
time, we had meetings with the people.

They had selected me as their business agent and passed around
my note pad requesting the collecting of dues. An election was held
by the state board. It was a union election concerning whether or
not the people wanted to be represented by a union. [The procedure
was specified by the Wagner Act of 1935.] The main union demand
we asked for was a 10% wage increase. At that time workers averaged about $20.00 a week. On the average, the wage increase meant
workers getting $2.00 more a week. We also asked that they grant
us a one week's vacation with pay. Prior to that, nobody had received a vacation with pay, no matter how long they'd worked for
the company. Some people had been working for the company fifty
years. There were no paid holidays, and we asked if they'd give us

They had selected me as their business agent and passed around my note pad requesting the collecting of dues. An election was held by the state board. It was a union election concerning whether or not the people wanted to be represented by a union. [The procedure was specified by the Wagner Act of 1935.] The main union demand we asked for was a 10% wage increase. At that time workers averaged about $20.00 a week. On the average, the wage increase meant workers getting $2.00 more a week. We also asked that they grant us a one week's vacation with pay. Prior to that, nobody had received a vacation with pay, no matter how long they'd worked for the company. Some people had been working for the company fifty years. There were no paid holidays, and we asked if they'd give us Christmas and Easter as two paid holidays. The company refused all of those demands, forcing us to go out on strike. Unable to successfully bargain for any kind of benefits, I immediately called a strike. We called a mass meeting first, the people voted to enter into the strike, and for seven weeks we were picketing the company for our demands. For seven weeks nobody was receiving any pay. There were hardly any welfare benefits at the time, and the business community was against the strike. We were villified and called Communists and radicals and everything else simply because we were trying to elevate the standard of living of the people.

There were no unions [among textile workers] to my knowledge at that time in Lowell. No unions at all. This was a new thing in the city. In order to support the union we used to hold tag days for various fund drives, and we were able to get a permit without a great deal of hassling with the city of Lowell. They gave us a permit to solicit money from people in the streets and give them a tag. They'd give us some coins in a box, and the tags would say: "We are supporting the strike at the Merrimack Manufacturing Company."

During the first seven weeks of the strike at the Merrimack they would bring trailer loads of so-called "scabs" [strikebreakers], people who meant well but didn't know the meaning of trade unionism. They were unemployed and had been unemployed all those years, and the company would go to New Hampshire and Vermont and bring these people in, load them in these trailer trucks, and try to bring them through the picket lines. In some cases they were successful; in other cases they were not successful. The violence was kept to a minimum because we were able to talk these people into not working and not hurting those who were out picketing for a decent living. But that was not very much of a problem in Lowell or in Lawrence and Haverhill and the other cities of

New England, but in the South there were professional scabs.
There were organizations that would employ scabs and hire them
out of these struck plants, and they would go in there. They were
rabble-rousers, and they would go there. They would work, and
they would taunt those who were out on strike and try to get them
to go back to work. In other words, they were trying to create the
impression -- the mill owners down there -- that the strike was
being broken and the cause was lost. If they wanted to preserve
their jobs, they should cross the picket lines.

Finally after seven weeks, the company acceded to our demands,
not because they wanted to, but because at that time Europe was
getting closer and closer to war and the company had orders from
the War Department to produce cloth and other orders from
France. And the United States Army and Navy were also contract-
ing at the time, and cloth was at a premium. So the government --
the goverments of these countries as well as the United States --
were pressuring the Merrimack Manufacturing Company for production. Out of necessity they capitulated. They granted the wage
increase, and we went back to work. That was my first experience
with the union. The following year, 1939, we struck again, and
again in 1940. We had three straight strikes.

Working conditions in the mills were the worst possible conditions that textile workers could work in. You couldn't see in front
of you for several hours for the steam, you worked close to thirteen
hours a day, and with maybe two or three inches of water all the
time on the floor. You had to wear boots in the dye house. The sanitary facilities were just unbelievable. The people working upstairs
in the spinning department worked with all kinds of foul matter,
and cotton lint was just all over the building. People were forced to
breath these cotton particles, which was injurious to their health.
In the weave room the noise was deafening. There was no protection for the ears as you have today. Today, in the spinning room
the air is filtered; in the dye room, we work on a dry floor. The
steam is only evident for the first few minutes of the working day.
The mill today is a far cry from the textile mill of the late Thirties.

Part of the demands aside from economic demands that we made
from the company was the conditions. See, we bargained collectively for employees for wages, hours of work, and conditions of employment and part of the conditions of being an employed worker
should be better working conditions. You could work in the mills if
you were sixteen. And I can remember people working there in

their late seventies and early eighties. The people who were unionized in the textile plants, they came from Greece, from Syria, from France and Canada, from Italy. They came here as teenagers at the turn of the century. And before the turn of the century they knew nothing else but working in a textile mill. And from the time that they came here in the 1880s and 1890s and worked forty and fifty years, they elevated their standard of living maybe three and a half to four dollars a week up to an average of about eighteen or nineteen or twenty dollars a week. But they were prone to layoffs. They lived in ghettos. There was a Polish ghetto, the Greek ghetto, the French-Canadian ghetto. The people lived in tenements; they lived in cold-water flats. When a man made fifteen to twenty dollars a week, he certainly didn't earn enough money to live decently. They didn't have a balanced diet; they lived on starches. As soon as the child became fifteen or sixteen years old, in order to be able to live decently, they had to force the child into working in the mill, getting a job so that they could have a decent standard of living. It's interesting that by the Thirties in Lowell especially, in Lawrence and Haverhill, and in the Northern cities, how many of the parents worked two or three jobs in order to afford their children an education. They would go without many things. They would do without proper clothing, without decently balanced diets in order to save enough money to send their children through high school and in many cases through college. There was no unemployment compensation at the time. There were no pensions at the time. There were no supplemental unemployment benefits as we have them today. No insurance, no health and welfare, no Blue Cross and Blue Shield at the time, and the layoffs were long, and in many cases seniority was not observed. Some were viewed as too old to produce what the mills considered the norm and, regardless of how many years of service you had, you were just thrown out on the scrap heap. One of the big fights we had with the employers over the years was to get them to agree to pay for a health insurance program, hospitalization, and surgical benefits. They were non-existent during those years, and after the war (in 1945 and 1946) we fought very hard, very strenuously to get the company to agree to the philosophy of paying for what is known today as Blue Cross and Blue Shield. For many years those plans were contributory. In other words, the company would pay half and the employee would pay half. But today the vast majority of the workers are covered by these plans which are fully paid by the employer.

My main occupation in the late Thirties was as a business agent of the union. I was getting $20.00 a week which included my expenses. I had an office where I was paying rent of $25.00 dollars a month, and I was bargaining collectively for the people. After several years we were able to get five paid holidays and a week and a half, close to two weeks vacation paid depending on how long you worked for the company. Then, of course, in 1941 we went into war. Because of the shortage of labor, wages automatically started to go up. And at that time my father had died, and I was the sole support of my younger brothers and my widowed mother. Under the Selective Service Act I was to be classified 3A and permitted to stay on and not be drafted into the service, so that I could support the younger children and my mother. But the draft board looked upon me as a radical, being a business agent of the union. So they were very, very happy to draft me in spite of what the law said. They drafted me and took me out of my job, but the union continued because I was succeeded by other people who were not of draft age. And that's how the union survived at the Merrimack Manufacturing Company. After the war I came back to the union. In 1945-46 the CIO (the Congress of Industrial Organizations) was coming into its own as a strong union, and they hired me as a business agent. And I worked for the CIO, organizing employees in areas I never knew, as well as in Lawrence and Haverhill and various other sections of New England.

In those years the people were afraid because the employer had created the impression in the minds of the worker that by joining the union there would be an automatic strike and you'd go out of work for many weeks and months without pay. Unions weren't welcomed in Lowell, they were anti-American, and unionism was something bad, was something vicious, and something completely un-American. They had been successful for many years making people believe this. There were many people who believed in unions. A lot of immigrants, people who had come from European countries, had some knowledge of unions because many of them had dealings with organizations long before they got here to America. They were familiar with what unions could do. The Polish-speaking people pretty much accepted the philosophy of the labor union, but the Anglo-Saxons pretty much resented it because they were convinced that it was an un-American thing. They called us all kinds of names including Communist. I was classified as a radical, and for a long long time that stigma stayed with me. When I finished my basic training, I had the I.Q. to qualify for Officers' Candidate School. But one of the first questions that was asked me when I went before the Officers' Candidate Board was what I thought of John L. Lewis [President of the CIO] and what I thought of labor organizers. I was being blackballed. They didn't want me to be an officer because of my background. Instead of asking me questions about the Army and about the things that I had studied to become an officer in the Army, they were asking me all kinds of questions about John L. Lewis, and about strikes, and about the mine workers, and about the steel workers, and about the auto workers. I told them at the time that, in my opinion, John Lewis had done more to alleviate the conditions of the miners than all the Congressmen all over the country that had ever been elected to Congress. And I could see that the Officers' Candidate Board would reject me, which they did.

The mills preferred to employ ethnic groups because in many instances the foreign, the so-called foreign-speaking people, spoke very little English. As a result of that they had very few complaints to make. They were the lowest people on the economic ladder. They were the only people who would work in the textile mills because if you had any sort of education and you spoke fluent English, you would try to keep away from the textile mill work. You would go into a shoe shop or another kind of a job that paid better wages and required a little better skill. For the most part foreigners had no skills, they came here from agrarian societies. And the only discrimination that I could see in the North as well as the South was the discrimination against black people. They would not hire black people at all with the exception of perhaps as janitors. In the South it was a double standard; a black man in the South made less wages than a white man even though they did a similar job. In many cases the union discriminated against the black down there because if you didn't do that you were considered pro-black and that would kind of slam the organization. The unions, in order to be successful in the South, in many cases practiced race prejudice. I'm talking about the late Forties and early Fifties when the unions were fairly strong, and they had the economic ability to support a strike by paying benefits to these people and giving them food. I can recall in many cases the black man would not be permitted to be in the line to collect these so-called commissary goods. He would have to wait and get the dregs. In all cases he was last, and in many cases there wasn't anything left for him.

In 1948 and 1949 I had been called upon to go to the South to organize the Southern workers who were very difficult to organize because of the great economic pressure that was exerted by the companies in the South. The very wealthy textile owners who controlled the towns, controlled the hospital, the police force, the fire department, the department stores that were in the town. And that made it extremely difficult for employees to organize.

Organizing in the South was a lot different from organizing, even at the very beginning, in Lowell because in the South, the state police would fight you, the local police would fight you if you tried to organize employees down there and hold meetings. The companies had spies and the state police. Company spies would come to the union hall and record the names of all those who attended the union meetings of the tentative organization. So it was a very, very tough thing. In many cases when we called strikes down there, half the people would come out on strike, the other half would be working. They would not permit us to picket peacefully. The Wagner Act gave us the right to picket and to organize, but the picketing was denied us. We were clubbed, the cottages we lived in were set on fire, many of us were beaten and put into jail. Organization was extremely slow for many, many years there.

The Ku Klux Klan played a major role together with the police and the town fathers in trying to keep the unions out of the South. As a union organizer, I can remember the Ku Klux Klan burning a cross for me and trying to beat me out of town. They tried at one time to burn the hotel that I lived in. The Klan slashed the tires on my car and stoned me. They did everything. They threatened to tar and feather me as they did to all the other labor leaders down there. In many cases the Ku Klux Klanners were the policemen in the town and the firemen. Also the foremen of the plant and, in many cases, workers that were scabbing.

Finally, I came back North and was stationed in Worcester in an administrative capacity. My organizational days were over. I was no longer organizing. I was negotiating contracts in those mills that had been organized for many years. I stayed with the CIO until I became a state director in Connecticut. In 1955, I resigned my position to become a labor arbitrator, arbitrating labor-management disputes. After several years of arbitrating I became a consultant specializing in labor relations.

THE FAMILY HISTORY OF SOPHIE AND THERESA

by Phyllis A. Stromvall

Sophie's Family History

As I relate the past eighty-two years of my life, or at least I think it was eighty-two, I try to think back and bring to life again the years I spent in Poland prior to my immigration to America. Life in Poland was simple and hard. Today, when you tell your grandchildren that you're not sure of your age, they look dumbfounded. It really wasn't easy to keep dates and ages in mind when your life consists of planting, tilling the soil, and doing household chores. Ages and dates mean little to you. And so, if you'll understand, I'll try to approximate as near as I am able to.

Life in Poland held few opportunities, but it was home -- a place where people understood you when you spoke. I think I was about eleven or twelve when I married my first husband. We lived in poverty, and that's all I ever knew. My husband worked in the salt mines where conditions were both straining and hazardous. We had a son, Joe, and not many years later, my husband contracted a lethal disease from the mines. He died shortly thereafter, and my son and I were left to live on what we could. When my neighbors offered me my passage to America, I decided to go -- I was sure life there would be much easier than in Poland. My sister also left with us, but my son did not come. I wanted to get established and find a job before taking him along, and also I did not have the money to pay for his passage. And so I left him with friends and promised to send for him within a very short time. I was sure I'd obtain a job that would in no time allow me to send for him and to provide us with a good life in America.

However, my image of America and America itself were completely different. I could not speak English, neither could I read or write. I was not treated very well because I was an illiterate; I almost hated to be here, but there was no way to go back to Poland. I never found a good job. I did work in the cotton mills in Lowell, but the pay was barely enough to survive on, the hours seemed endless, and the conditions were at the most bearable. My sister and I both worked in the mills; being illiterate and foreigners, we knew no one nor were we accepted by many. Many of the other mill workers were also immigrants -- most kept to their own kind. We were frightened, disillusioned, and hopelessly poor. Our food consisted of the cheapest food available -- potatoes, bread, and some vegetables were the main diet. I thought constantly of my son and my promise to him, but the money was never saved to bring him over. Our wages were poor in comparison to the work we did to earn them. The factory was dark and filthy; in the winter it was very cold, and our hands would nearly freeze. There was no real heat, and it was either work or starve, and so I tried to bear my job as best I could. In the summer it was just the opposite; the heat was so intense that we would drench our bodies with our perspiration. The seasons were rough in America; like in Poland, the winters were bitterly cold and the snow accumulation averaged higher than it does today. We thought many times of the old country and we compared it to life here; there was not a great deal of difference between the two. Over here we were wretched immigrants, who were cheap labor and easily manipulated. Over in Poland we were starving citizens who had nothing.

There were other Polish immigrants in the factory -- one in particular whose name was Stanley. In those days there was no fancy courting as such; we never had money to go places or to buy gifts. We were both in similar situations, and so we married one another. I left the mills to live with Stanley, and we moved to what is now Pawtucketville. The apartment was small and run down, but it was a home away from the mills and the city district. The area was virtually unsettled, as there were only five other houses in the neighborhood. But there was land on which to grow vegetables, and we could eat better than we had previously. Stanley began to work as a wool sorter, and he walked the three and one half miles

every day to his job; I made a tiny garden at home and grew potatoes and cabbages and a few other vegetables. Our life was by no
means good, but it was better. Our neighbors were mostly Greeks,
and they could not speak English either. But we were all friends, because we had all undergone a change in life style and were still
living as immigrant Americans. All of our neighbors worked in the
mills -- we had no trades or skills and there were no jobs that were
open to us. We were looked upon as nothing; indeed even our
names meant little to the non-immigrant Americans we dealt with.
In City Hall they spelt our names according to how they thought
they should be spelled -- Stanley's name did not even resemble the
present family name. They spelled our name as they heard it, not as
it was.

Two years after we were married, we had our first child, a girl.
We named her Christina and she was very precious to me, as she
symbolized the connecting link between ourselves and America.
She would be brought up to speak English and thus translate for
us. I brought her up in my own way, teaching her our language
(which she picked up readily) and preparing her to alleviate the
burden in the home. She was especially favored because I had lost
my son; I knew even then that there would be little chance of ever
bringing him to America. Now, I had a child to console my grief --
by this time I had long since stopped sending money to my son in
Poland and only wrote to him occasionally. He was being raised by
friends in Poland; he would never know of any other life than that.

When Chris was about four, we had a second child, Helen. I did
love her, of course, but by then I had been accustomed to spoiling
Chris and doing everything for her. I was somewhat disappointed
in that I had wanted a son rather than another daughter. You see,
girls grow up and get married and leave their mothers; a boy
would stay with his mother and support her. If Stanley died I
would be left alone; with a son, he could work and support me for
the rest of my life.

When World War I broke out, Stanley was too old to go into the
service. He was then about thirty-five, and they didn't take many
older men. And so, for this reason the war did not affect us in any
drastic way. Stanley was still working, and the money continued to
come home. I managed as best as I could on his small pay. We were
by no stretch of the imagination prosperous, but we lived better
than those who lived in the cities because we had land. It wasn't
our land, but it was good productive soil and it provided us with a

fairly balanced diet. We ate little meat; the price for meat was just too high, and it couldn't be stretched as far as vegetables could. Besides that, there was no way to keep food refrigerated. Much of our winter food was canned; I prepared beets, pickles, tomatoes, corn relish, and fruits. Vegetables such as potatoes and cabbage were either chopped up and prepared in a crock for sauerkraut or they were kept, along with carrots and beans, in a storage bin with sand. And so by the time the Twenties rolled around, we were still struggling to maintain a decent standard of living.

During the Twenties the mills in Lowell were beginning to decline. Stanley continued to work but we never obtained the wealth that others had. We walked anywhere we went; cars were a dream to us. It was at the beginning of this decade that my son was born. We named him Joseph; indeed, here was my hope for the future. He would go to school and become a smart, hard-working boy who would care for his mother and stay with her as long as she needed him.

Chris was already growing up. She had been in school a few years and was able to teach me some English. My husband acquired some English in the mills, where he encountered all types of people. Joey was my lost son re-born to me; I finally found consolation for the boy who was mine back in Poland. When my last child, Stella, was born two years later, I had to go out and look for extra work to help support the family. [Sophie and Chris did seasonal agricultural labor, picking strawberries.]

It was during this time that Stanley began to drink heavily. Every payday he would stop off at a barroom and get drunk before coming home. In spite of prohibition laws, the local taps were able to keep the customers well supplied. His visits to the bar began to get more and more frequent; most of his pay went to the support of his habit. What was left of his pay was many times stolen from him by the bartenders or his drinking companions. They knew that a few shots would do it for him, and at times they would buy him a round just to keep him drunk. As his habit increased, so did his temper. He would become enraged when he was drunk and got into a good many brawls in the bar. He was well known throughout the neighborhood, both as a drunk and as a family-beater. When he came home drunk, he usually took his anger out on us. My children and I never escaped his beatings -- we were terrified of him. He thought nothing of us as he drank more often; many weeks I'd get nothing with which to buy food. The children and I have never forgotten this. To be ill-treated by strangers is one thing but to be ill-treated by your own husband and father is another. To escape his strong and powerful hands, we slept in the woods many nights. Even during the winter it was not uncommon to find us huddling in the snow. We preferred freezing to being beaten. We were frostbitten and hungry. Chris and Helen were anxious to leave home to escape the nightmare. I needed my son to hold our family together and to replace the husband who had to do this. Stanley could never repair the damage he did to us. He was tough and strong and would fight with anyone who stepped in his way. But he could not stay sober and provide support for us. He decided instead to drink.

And so, by the time the Depression hit, our family had changed quite a lot. Chris had married and moved closer to the city by this time. Helen had also married a young Irishman who seem ambitious and prosperous. I had since decided that I no longer wished to live with my husband, and so he moved out. Joey and Stella were the only ones left at home, and since they were only ten and eight years old, I was forced to seek work. Again, I went back to the mills and did whatever jobs I could. I was determined not to suffer as I had with my husband, but I was also determined not to be left adrift again.

Joey and Stella went to the neighborhood school. The two-roomed Lexington Avenue School consisted of two floors, each floor containing a room with two grade levels. The entire neighborhood attended this school. The walk was a short one compared to the walks to the other schools. Joey was the only one of my four children that took a real liking to school; my girls preferred to get married and keep house.

When the Depression was finally a reality, I lost my job and with it the money to buy food. We had nothing before and nothing now. Faced with starvation we began to eat anything that was consumable; during the summer, dandelion greens were our diet; during the winter we ate hard bread, sweetened with sugar if we were that lucky. Everywhere people starved, raiding garbage to keep alive. Our neighbors were no better off than we were -- no one worked. It was useless for the children to quit school; at least there they could keep warm and stay clear of the streets and alleys. At home there was one tiny stove that had to heat the house. It gave off little comfort and warmth, but the fuel to run it was hard to get. Joey and Stella would walk for miles to the tracks, hoping along with many others, to collect some coal in a wagon to bring it home. Our only income was from Joe's paper route. The trouble was most of his customers couldn't afford to pay him every week. Many weeks he wouldn't earn anything; other weeks he'd receive only a few cents. I re-made their clothes so many times that they just became threadbare. Their shoes were stuffed with newspapers to protect their feet from freezing altogether. By the Depression, both Joe and Stella had graduated to the Bartlett Junior High School which was over two miles across the river. They walked to school every day, being grateful for the heat they did not have at home. One by one, our neighbors began to lose their homes. The banks foreclosed the mortgage and put the houses up for bid. Many times they were able to remain in their houses, due to the fact that no one could afford to buy the houses. Our water was shut off as the unpaid bills began to mount. As each family was notified of the shut-off, they would fill up bathtubs, pails, sinks and any container they could spare to get the water before it was shut off. If we washed our bodies it was only with cold water; most times we weren't able to spare the water. Stanley lost his job also, but he did not come back to live with us.

My married children were more fortunate than us. Chris and her husband had managed to save some money, and Ted was able to work every now and then. Helen too was able to get by. Her husband Eddy worked and was able to get them through the Depression on a little better than subsistance level. They obtained credit at a local market which supplied them with a good deal of food. Eddy was able to work and support his family, and they managed to help Chris and her family out when they needed it.

But for us it was another story. We survived through the bread lines, which meant sometimes a twelve to thirteen hour wait. We were apportioned what was considered an "equal lot." Most of the time the portions were inherently unequal. People like us who were poor and powerless received nothing. Those who knew someone or the person who gave out the food always got more. It was not unusual for us to walk away empty-handed. Pity and sympathy were emotions that these officials hid; how they could knowingly refuse a person food to give it to someone else was beyond our understanding. Most nights we went to bed early, about five or six o'clock. Many nights we went to bed without any supper; every night we slept with our clothes on. We had one blanket; we never even pretended that it kept us warm. We had to go to bed early -- there was no other way to try to keep warm when the sun went down. In the mornings, especially during the winter, we dressed up under the covers. The house was so cold that if we awoke during the night or early morning to urinate, we didn't, because it was just too cold.

We were ashamed, discouraged, desperate; I almost never had the money to supply the children with a decent lunch for school. Most of the time they took bread; if there was no hard bread, they took nothing. They relied on begging, borrowing or doing without. Joey and his friends would sometimes go to the place where the Sunday communion hosts were made; whatever scraps weren't used were salvaged by them and eaten.

In spite of the rough times we had one and only one consolation -- everyone else was as bad off as we were. The only seasons that kept us from starving were spring and summer. We ate, as I said, dandelions, berries, grape leaves, mushrooms (if we could find some to pick) and some vegetables. On rare occasions we would sell something we owned to buy a little meat. Although we suffered with the heat, the summer was much easier to bear than the winter. The Merrimack River had long been the favorite bathing spot; there was a beach and a bath house and people swarmed to the river as much as they could. It also served as an ice rink during the winter, for those fortunate enough to own skates. Joe built his own out of wood. Given the materials, he could build just about anything.

And the Depression wore on. Finally, when the paper route was costing us rather than paying us, Joey went out to look for a job. He had by this time graduated from Bartlett Junior High and had given up all of his hopes of continuing school and becoming a lawyer. He was my only son, and we depended on him to support us. He was fifteen and able to work, and we needed money desperately. Of course, there were hundreds of others in Lowell who were also seeking jobs. He searched for months, always coming away frustrated. At one particular factory on Bridge Street in Lowell, he was promised that the employer would consider him. Determined to get the job, he walked the four or five miles everyday, just to sit in the waiting room all the while hoping the employer would notice him. But he didn't; in fact, he pointedly ignored him. Joe, however, refused to give up. He knew I was depending on him; he walked to that factory no matter the weather for a solid month. After a month of this ordeal had gone by, the employer suddenly spoke to Joe. He said, "You've been here everyday for an entire

A familiar sight in downtown Lowell during the Depression
(Library of Congress)

month. You must really want the job." "I do want the job," answered Joe. "I'm willing to do any kind of work." The man gave him the job. "Come back tomorrow at six o'clock." "How about my starting now?" Joe asked. The employer agreed to it, and Joey worked until eleven o'clock that night. At home we were worried sick; I had no idea that he was working. When the hours began to get later, I was sure something terrible had happened to him. By the time he got home it was early morning; he was exuberant. He had finally gotten the job. They had let him work, and he had to be back for six o'clock that morning. I hadn't felt this good in a long time.

Eventually, his boss began to get more and more demanding. He expected Joe to work two or three shifts sometimes and besides expected his production rates to increase. Jobs were becoming a little more available, and Joe found one in the iron works. He quit his factory job and accepted one that was even more strenuous. He and the other men worked hacking away and removing heavy pipes, metal and whatever else was demanded of them. Joe remembers how he was treated more like a slave than an employee. The boss walked up and down the rows of men, surveying their work and their speed. Water buckets were kept nearby but to drink water meant to stop and waste time and this was not what the boss was paying them for. The boss, although it sounds barbaric, carried a whip in his hand and was free in his use of it. One particular day he accused Joey of making too many trips to the water bucket. When he threatened to "smarten him up," Joey nearly flattened him. He was capable of beating this boss to a pulp, and the boss knew it; he left Joe alone after that. But the work never lessened. He would come home nights with his back bent and so sore that he could neither sit nor lie down. But the boss never cared; he was making a handsome profit on the sweat of others.

And then came 1936. The winter was a bitterly cold one, even though we didn't have a great deal of snow. As the spring approached, we found that our land was still very deeply frozen. Since we lived near the Merrimack, we kept a watchful eye on its level. Stella had just gotten married to a young Italian, Paul. He was ambitious, attractive, aggressive -- we knew he would go far. They moved upstairs from Joey and me, and so I never really lost her. But all my children except for Joey had gone off, married, and left their mother. Even though Joe was only eighteen, he showed no signs of being interested in girls. He was good to me; he never would leave me on my own. My husband, we heard, was managing without us. I didn't really miss him a great deal; his drunken brutality had continued to haunt me and my children. But we had other things to worry about. A flood seemed inevitable; the land was just not thawing to absorb the melting snows from the northern mountains. With the spring came the flood warning -- we were told to evacuate our homes. Where were we supposed to go? There was nowhere to go. And then the flood came. Dams broke and the Merrimack swelled, its waters rising so high that it washed bridges away with it. The bridges at both Bridge Street and Thorndike Street were completely washed away. Entire homes were covered over. It hit our house, which was built on an incline. We brought whatever clothing and food we could up to the attic and lived there. The water reached the second story of the house, burying all the furniture in its freezing foam. Our neighbors had evacuated their homes; no one knew we were still living in ours. Joe and Paul would swim underwater into Stella's apartment and try to salvage any food they could find in the refrigerator. We lived like this for well over a week, isolated from everyone and everything. The flood was so powerful that it completely overwhelmed us. The Bridge Street Bridge was completely washed away, and the city was divided into small isolated areas similar to islands. We were at our wits' end, wondering how life could get any worse. The Depression was still on, and now whatever we did have was for the most part lost. During our stay in the attic we weren't even able to keep a fire going, for fear of it spreading. For nights on end, we had to combat both the cold and the unshakable fear that we would never survive. After our severe isolation, it was necessary for Joey and Paul to go out; they had kept a rowboat in the attic for this purpose. As they floated about in the water, they contended with the power lines -- the waters had risen to just below the power lines. For weeks we endured this devastating flood, with only the high land areas or the parts of the city such as Hale and Howard streets, escaping the tremendous waters. By the time the waters subsided and we could move back into the house proper, the damage had already done its deed. Our furniture was half rotted, any tools or metal pieces were rusted and corroded, and we had to start at the beginning all over again.

Never will I forget the Depression years and all the misery it brought to us; my children will always have the feeling that they lost their childhood and were forced to mature too quickly. Whatever misery I had experienced in Poland was equaled by my life in America. Experiences such as these are never forgotten.

With the threat of war, I again went back to work in the mills. My son Joe decided to enter the service and went to volunteer for the Navy. They refused him stating he had flat feet and a bad back, but the Army welcomed him. He left me in December of 1941 and was gone for a good many years. Stella's husband Paul was also in the service. Helen's husband Eddy had at this time bought himself a barroom with a partner and was doing quite well -- they also had quite a large family with their seven children. Chris' husband Ted also went to war; few people escaped.

Joey was gone for four long years. I struggled at home as best I could, but the bills just weren't being paid. I could not keep up with the rent payments on the house, and so the owner decided to sell. I would end up in the street with no money and no house. I wrote to Joey quickly, telling him I needed close to $1,000 down payment if I was to buy the house and remain in it. Two weeks later the money came; he had bet everything he owned gambling and had won. That's how he was able to send as much money home as he did. Occasionally he would gamble in poker and with a little skill and a lot of luck, he won. I was able to buy the house and worry no more about landlords or overdue rent. Joey would pay the mortgage, and I would stay in my house. When the war ended Joe came home.

With his arrival home he began to make plans for improving and re-building the house. It was around this time that he met his future wife, Theresa. She was one of Stella's friends and occasionally would come over and visit. Joey was painfully shy of her, as he was of many girls; he had never actually dated any although there were many who wished to date him. Finally, he got enough courage to invite her out. They appeared to get along fairly well. She was a fairly attractive girl, very shy herself. She was Italian and came from the Howard Street district of Lowell. We didn't know all that much about her. Her parents had both immigrated from Italy.

Theresa's father had come over first to settle down and find a job, and later he sent for his wife. They had four children in America including Theresa and had not been able to manage very well. Her father Salvatore worked whenever he could, but many times he had no job. They lived in one of the tenement houses, and to get money they hired one of their rooms out for boarders. They had lived in the Italian district with many of their Italian "paisans" or friends. The gathering place for their neighbors was the Italian Club on Central Street. The atmosphere that Terry grew up in was

quite different from the one that Joey grew up in. Life in the city
meant no trees or land or, for that matter, privacy. The tenements
were packed in close together and weren't kept up by the landlords.
The only English most of the old country people heard was from
their school-age children.

Terry's parents struggled to keep alive in the city. They were
strict, old-fashioned immigrants who believed in solid respect for
the elders and in a strong attachment to Italian customs. The two
girls, Nicoletta and Theresa, were forced to keep their hair long;
their father, Salvatore refused to allow their hair to be cut. In spite
of the hot, humid summers and the humiliation his daughters felt,
he would not give in. The current style was short, wavy hair; for
his daughters, it was long, straight hair. The children were not allowed to chew gum or (heaven forbid) smoke. Salvatore was the
ruler of the family. His wife Maria was not quite as strict, but she
too required obedience and respect from their children. All four
children attended the area public schools and were warned to be
wary of people who weren't Italian. Salvatore found his nationality
a stigma many times in seeking employment. He feared for his
children and the torment they would have to endure; he was
proud to be an Italian, but harrassed because of it in America.

In school, Theresa was a painfully shy girl. She had few friends
other than her neighbors, and both she and her sister and brothers
were passed over by many teachers for the better off Irish and
Jewish students. The teachers favored the "rich kids" and neglected
the others. Theresa never did very well in school, because she
found it difficult to adjust to the environment of the school. She
and her sister were very often ridiculed because they owned only
two dresses and their shoes were stuffed with newspapers. It was
embarrassing for them to wear the same clothes until they were
threadbare, while others claimed an entire wardrobe of clothes.
Their clothes were old-fashioned; their hair was not stylish; they
had no money. They found that life treated some people better than
others. Life was rough for them. They ate whatever they could,
which was a great deal of hard bread and macaroni. Meat consisted
of turkey and chicken necks, that were first boiled for soup stock
and then eaten. Once a year Maria bought a chicken, not a turkey,
for Christmas dinner. Then it seemed much of the remainder of the
year was spent paying for the chicken.

Salvatore lost his job during the Depression, and the family
relied on boarders, the bread lines, and a newspaper route to keep

themselves alive. They lived like us only worse. They lived beside neighbors who didn't lose out when the crash came and who were still able to maintain a decent style of living. Salvatore and Maria could give their children nothing. At Christmas time, the only gifts they ever received were from their landlord -- Terry's first and only doll was given to her by the landlord. Terry's brother, Dominic was the only child who was able to attend and complete high school. Being the youngest family member, he was cared for more protectively than the others. Nicky and Terry, the oldest, were ex-pected to help the family out if they could find a job. But for the lon-gest time there were no jobs.

During the summers when school wasn't in session, Salvatore managed to rent a piece of land to grow a garden. However, the land had been a dump heap. Barrels upon barrels of garbage had to be cleared, and the dry soil needed to be cultivated and broken. The soil was not very good, but it was suitable for planting certain vegetables. By going into debt, they were able to buy some seeds and begin their gardening. Salvatore constructed a hose that led the water to the garden and was attached to a crude pump. One child would work the pump, and the others would carry pails from the pump to the soil and back again. They sweated and toiled from dawn to night in their wretched garden. Many of their neighbors regarded their activity as fruitless labor, but when the autumn came that first year, the garden had produced enough food to store for the winter months. Some of it did have to be sold to pay for the rent on the land, but there was food to save and eat later. At this point, many of their neighbors attempted to beg off much of their harvest. Theresa recalled that "suddenly my father had many friends." He could never refuse a fellow "paisan," and so some of their hard-earned food was given away. But not that much. Salva-tore did not forget the fact that he and his children sweated alone and that many of his neighbors viewed him as a fool. Every summer after that, food began to get stolen from their garden. Jea-lous and hateful neighbors would help themselves to vegetables as the crops began to ripen. Salvatore had no way to protect the prop-erty, save for staying there day and night. They guarded what they could but always lost a great deal of their harvest.

Salvatore became a citizen of the United States about the time that Franklin Roosevelt became President in 1933. During Roose-velt's first term in office, Salvatore began to work for the WPA, and this, more than anything else, brought renewed life back to him and his family. To the family who had had nothing all their lives,

Roosevelt meant a new life to them. They were bitter toward Herbert Hoover and his "chicken for every pot" slogan; they saw the Republican Party as an organization that ignored the poor and helped to further the rich. Roosevelt created Salvatore's first real job; in return, Salvatore and his family would support Roosevelt and praise him almost as they would a saint. To them the WPA meant money and the ability to live decently.

When Roosevelt was elected for a second term in 1936, the family was able to make a bill and buy a radio. Salvatore had voted for Roosevelt and had a great deal of confidence in him. To them the radio meant a connection with American society. It was a treasured article in their home and their only link with the life style of the prosperous Americans. In 1938, Theresa graduated from the Morey Junior High School, and she joined her sister Nicky in the working world. She began to work for a Jewish family doing what was supposed to be light housework for ten cents a week. She worked every day except Sunday, although her employer tried to persuade her to work Sunday also. This was her first actual experience in dealing with the middle class. Her employer was a Jewish businessman, and he and his wife had three children of various ages. The wife was a lazy, fussy and highly demanding woman -- she hated housework but was very critical of Terry's work. She knew that she could exploit Terry because the Depression was still on and there were few jobs. Theresa worked from eight in the morning to eight at night, but many nights she worked until midnight or later. She not only did housework, but ended up minding the children, preparing some meals, doing some of the shopping, running errands and anything else that her employer demanded. If her employers went out for the night, as they frequently did, she was left to feed the children and to put them to bed. Nicky also worked for a Jewish woman, who was a kinder and more considerate employer. Occasionally she received some food as a sort of bonus or reward. Nicky didn't mind as much to work for the Jews; Theresa hated it.

Theresa worked for this family for three years; within that time she had acquired a deep and lasting hatred for them. When Roosevelt was elected to his third term in 1940, she begged to quit her job, for she could no longer stand the ordeal of working late and being treated roughly. Her employer began to criticize her work more severeley and to punish Theresa when she saw fit. On one particular night, Theresa waited at the house until 2:00 a.m. with nothing to eat. Then she left before her employers came home, an action she had never done before. She ran home and begged her father to let her quit; he agreed to it. When the woman found her absent that morning, she went to Terry's house and demanded an explanation. Theresa told her flatly that she would never work for her again.

When World War II was finally declared, new jobs in the mills opened up. Nicoletta began to work for Prince Macaroni. Through the aid of a friend of her father's, Theresa was able to get a job as unskilled labor in one of the cotton mills. She said the only way one could get a job in the mills at the time was if someone you knew spoke up for you. This friend was a foreman and so was able to get her a job. Their brother Vincent did odd jobs, attempting to pick up a trade. Dominic, the youngest, had graduated from high school at the onset of World War II and began a job in one of the local grocery markets.

Within the first two years of war, Salvatore died of a sudden heart attack. Their mother Maria never worked and so relied now on her children for support. The war was good to them because it meant jobs and prosperity, but Vincent was drafted and served in the Army, and Dominic eventually went also as the war dragged on and the need for men became greater. Dominic was able to go to Italy and visit the relatives of his mother. They were starving and poor, and they begged him to pay for their passage to America. He promised them that he'd do what he could, but it was impossible to gather the money to bring any of them over and to provide for housing and jobs for them.

Eventually, the only ones left at home were Maria and her two daughters. In 1944 she died. The girls became the heads of the house. They continued to work, and when the war ended the two boys came home, and the four remained together. Then Theresa met Joey and began to date him. They got married in 1946. The two family histories became one family history.

Theresa's Family History

During most of the two and a half years that I went with Joe before our marriage, his mother was fond of me. She did not see me as stealing her son away from her. She viewed me, rather, as a hard working "good" girl. I expected her to give Joe a hard time when he began to date me, but she didn't.

At first I found it very difficult to adjust to a new atmosphere --
Polish foods and customs were strange to me. I really didn't like
Polish food at all -- Italian food is spicy and made with macaroni
and tomatoes; Polish food is bland and made with potatoes, cabbage and milk. The first Christmas I went with Joe, he invited me to
have the Polish feast with his family on Christmas Eve. There I met
his sisters and their husbands. I was very nervous about both the
food and the people I was to meet, and so I was ill and embarrassed.
It took me a long time to get used to the Polish foods and customs.
We hadn't had the Italian Christmas feast since my mother died.
Needless to say, the Polish life was difficult for me to adjust to. But I
had to adjust if I was to make a good wife for Joe. He observed all
the customs and loved the food; he wanted me to learn to cook it as
well as develop a taste for it.

I was still working at the mills when I met Joe. The work never
bothered me but I was always uncomfortable with the people I
worked with. The women were catty, two-faced and jealous -- we
did piece work and there was always contention and jealousy over
certain jobs. I always looked young for my age, and when I first
began to work at the mills, the workers believed that I had lied
about my age and was not actually sixteen. They also accused me of
being a brown-nose, a term that we used on some of the kids at
school. The bosses in the mills were the kind that could easily be
persuaded to grant favors if given what they wanted. There was a
lounge they called the smoking room, where many of the workers
would spend their coffee breaks and lunch hours, telling dirty
jokes. It was a rough crowd at the mills, and I wanted no part of
them. I would simply mind my business and do my work, very glad
when each day was over. Unlike most of the women there I would-
n't give the bosses what they wanted -- some of the married
women got pregnant by the bosses. However, minding my business
and doing my work got me nowhere; the aggressive women always
got the best jobs and raises.

After Joey and I were engaged and began to make plans for the
wedding, we decided to live in Joe's house with his mother. The
idea sounded wonderful at the time, for his mother would be able
to help cook and clean the house while I worked. When they asked
me about our plans at work and I told them that we'd live with
Joe's mother, they tried to persuade me not to do it. Everyone told
me I'd be sorry. I wouldn't listen to any of them. Joe's mother likes
me, things are different with us, I'd tell them. But they continued to
warn me. I thought that they were just talking nonsense, for I got

along beautifully with his mother. When I had first begun to work at the mills I bought something every week to put away for when I got married. By the time we did get married I had accumulated quite a lot of things. Everything seemed to be going so well.

Then, as the wedding grew nearer, Joe's mother became more hostile toward me. She tried to stop the wedding and accused me of being no good. Her daughter Stella told her stories about me that weren't true. I was hesitant about moving in with her, but Joe convinced me that everything would go smoothly. Besides, he argued, he was still responsible for his mother, and he would not turn her out of his house. I had no parents to help me out or advise me; my sister Nicky was just as confused as I was. In the end I convinced myself that once we were married, Joe's mother would change her attitude toward me. But I was completely mistaken; she changed, but she grew worse. She resented the fact that I would handle the household money, not her. She claimed it was her house (which it wasn't), and she had always managed the bills until I took over. We had thought that we would be able to save some money and fix up the house more than what we had been able. After we got married his mother handed me a stack of bills that she had made under Joe's name, saying that since she could handle the money no longer, she would no longer pay her bills. It was our responsibility now. She upset me very much; every penny we had saved went to pay her bills. She would do no housework or cooking while I was at work but waited for me to come home and do it all. When she was in a rare mood, she washed clothes and sometimes ironed hers and Joey's (never mine). Most of the time she was a complete dictator. She made me iron and wash clothes as soon as I came home -- before supper. I hated her and she hated me; Joey always stayed neutral. He would never defend me or anything I did, and his mother began to cry to his sisters about her terrible daughter-in-law. I had first his mother to contend with, and then his sister Stella and her husband Paul. Joe's father Stanley had moved next door to us in a shack of a house, and Joe's sister Chris was forever over at our house, eating supper with us and visiting her mother.

For three long years I endured his mother. I begged my husband countless times to give the house to his mother and move out on our own. Many times I threatened to leave, but I never did. I hated the idea of his mother running our house and inviting her other children to eat the food she had never bought. Paul and Stella were living upstairs from us and paying no rent. This made me furious, because Paul had gotten a job as a police officer and was doing quite well.

Just before we were married, Joe had gotten a job as an orderly at a nearby Veteran's Administration Hospital; after six months they promised him a job in recreation, where there was an opening. We were thrilled, because recreation was the field Joe wanted. We weren't married a year before Joe had an interview for the depart- ment. However, when he filled out the form, they notice that he wasn't a high school graduate. "I'm a self-made man," Joe told them. But they refused him. Joe became quite upset and told them, "You can take your job and pound it, because if all you care about is a piece of paper, then I don't want your lousy job." He stormed out of the office and went back to his job. The next day he received a call saying he had the job in recreation -- they liked his "spunk" as they called it.

During our first few years of marriage we began to fix up the house, concentrating on the yard first. We also had a beautiful site for a garden -- so we cleared off the top level and turned up beauti- ful rich soil for gardening. We planted many vegetables, which helped out alot financially. At this time the electric chest freezers were coming out -- we decided to buy one, which would enable us to buy meat on sale and freeze it for later use and to freeze our garden vegetables. His mother refused to eat the frozen meat and accused us of trying to poison her. She told this to all her daughters, and they too criticized us for freezing food. It seemed as though I couldn't stand it much longer -- I was exhausted from trying to work and keep up a house, and I was emotionally worn out dealing with his mother.

We had no car and relied on buses for our transportation. I would have to do my food shopping downtown after work, and then I would have to carry the bulky shopping bags home with me. The bus line ended about a quarter of a mile from our house. The bags would be ripped and my arms would be broken by the time I finally reached our home. When I did, I would have to listen to his mother, who never did anything but complain.

Finally, the time came for her to move out. My sister-in-law Stella, had bought a house and invited my mother-in-law to live with her. It came at an opportune time for Stella, because Sophie was just beginning to receive Social Security checks. She also wished to move away from her husband Stanley, who lived next

door to us. I was then expecting my first baby, and my mother-
in-law's room was to be used as a nursery. So with the onset of the
Korean war, Joey's mother moved out and we had our first baby,
Ann-Marie.

Now that we were parents and landlords, we decided to improve
our house and settle down to live here. We rented the upstairs
apartment to Joe's niece and her husband for a minute amount of
money. Little by little, we fixed up rooms in the house and tilled
the yard to plant grass. It was also an important time because we
bought our first car, a blue 1951 Ford. Joey no longer had to pay for
rides to work, but also was able to take a passenger or two himself.
The car was a blessing for us -- we were able to go places and not
be confined to the house. I quit my job at the mill when Ann-Marie
was born, and our little family made use of our new car for picnics
and day trips. We began to go places that we had never been; it
seemed as though a whole new world was being opened up to us.

Two years after Ann-Marie was born, we had our second daughter, Kathy. Our five-room house began to be a little cramped as our
family expanded. My sister-in-law Stella and Paul also had a
daughter, a month before mine was born. Shortly after that Paul
died suddenly of a heart attack. My mother-in-law became indis-
pensable to Stella, acting as both mother and homemaker for her --
Stella became a woman police officer because of her husband's
death. She later married a man whom she met in a drug store in the
area where she directed traffic. They did marry, but the Catholic
Church never recognized their marriage because Joe, her husband,
was divorced.

In 1956 our last child, Janet was born. Our house was just too
small to accomodate five people. We had only two bedrooms, and
one was so tiny that a double-bed and a bureau barely fit in. At one
point we decided to sell the house and buy another. Some friends of
ours who lived farther up the avenue were interested in selling to
us -- the house was immense. There was plenty of land with a
large shed and coop and the house had large rooms on both the top
and lower floors. We were anxious to buy but we didn't -- we just
couldn't afford the taxes and the mortgage at the time. We did look
into several new homes but the prices at the time seemed high;
today, those same prices for a brand new home are considered a
"steal"; and this wasn't so long ago either -- merely ten or eleven
years.

It turned out that of my family, only my brother Vinnie and I married. Vinnie and his wife never had any children. My sister Nicky had gone with someone for quite a few years, but he became interested in another when she turned down his proposal. My brother Dominic was quite interested in Joe's niece, but she regarded him only as a friend, and nothing more. Nicky and Dominic continued to live on Howard Street after my brother Vinnie married. Nicky continued to work at Prince Macaroni, and Dominic had obtained a job at Stop and Shop food stores. They lived on Howard Street many, many years. They liked the district until it became too shabby and dirty. About ten years ago, they bought themselves a brand new home up the street from us -- my sister cried when she left Howard Street; in fact, the night she moved in her new home, she wanted to go back to her apartment and sleep on the bare floors.

As the girls began to grow into their teens, we began to expand our home, by adding on two large bedrooms, a half bath, a hallway and a back porch. Joey built the entire addition himself with some help from us. In fact everything he did in repairing the house, he did himself. From the time the girls started school, Joey and I emphasized the need for an education for them. From their elementary school days they spoke of college and what they would become. All three of our girl's attended Lexington Avenue School, the grade school Joey attended. When it came time for high school, Ann-Marie chose to attend Keith Hall. Kathy decided to attend Lowell High. Now both attend Lowell State College for diverse careers and our youngest, Janet, goes to Lowell High.

The last ten years have seen many changes in our life; Joey's father has since passed away, his mother now is cared for in a nursing home, Joey has been promoted in his department -- he now directs recreation programs for all the family care units and nursing homes of veterans within this area of the state. Our home now looks completely different from the original one, and we've been able to travel both in the U.S. and in Canada. We've been camping now for almost ten years. With cars and trailers and highways, we're able to get away and see the places we've always wanted to see. Our eldest daughter is now married, and our middle daughter is engaged. We've seen old neighbors move and new ones come in -- the avenue has expanded so that it looks more like the outskirts of the city rather than the country. We've seen wars, including Vietnam, and we've watched as this country has had both great and poor leaders. We've been staunch Democrats and believers in the people, not in business. Today [in 1973] as we heard of Governor Wallace's shooting, we paused and reflected on the future of this country. From dirt poverty, we came to lead a fairly good life -- we've seen a lot of hard times and a lot of good times. I don't regret any of it.

GLOSSARY

back-boy   assistant to the mule spinner whose major jobs included keeping the mules supplied with roving to be spun while sweeping and cleaning the area.

beamer   operator in a process by which warp threads are wound onto a beam which fits into a power loom for weaving.

blacklist   the gathering by management of names of troublesome employees (usually union activists) in order to deny them employment and access to other workers in the mill.

bummer   derogatory term for strikebreakers during the mule spinners' strike of 1875.

carder   operator of a carding machine which both cleans the cotton, separates the fiber, and arranges the cotton into a soft tubular roll or sliver.

craft or trade union   an organization whose membership is reserved for workers possessing skill in a particular trade, usually acquired through an apprenticeship.

doffer   the job of removing full bobbins, replacing them with empty ones, and restarting the spinning machine.

filling   yarn which runs at right angles or across the length-wise warp threads in woven fabric.

industrial union   an organization whose membership is extended to any worker, whatever level of skill, who labors in a particular industry.

lockout   action take by management to shut down a mill in order to deny employment to workers.

loom fixer   skilled mechanic assigned to keep power looms functioning properly.

make a bill   purchase on credit.

mule   mule spinning machine.

napper   operator of a finishing machine which gives a soft surface to cotton cloth such as flannel.

nobstick   see **bummer**.

picker   operator of a picking machine, the initial process of opening and cleaning cotton fiber from the bale.

Sampas-coopies   a newspaper column of local history and anecdotes written by Charles G. Sampas for the *Lowell Sun* between 1938 and 1976.

slasher-tender   operator of a machine which applies starch or size to a sheet of warp yarns.

speed-up   altering the speed of machines or the pace of work with no additional pay.

stretch-out   assigning additional work or machines with no additional pay.

strikebreaker   a worker who knowingly accepts employment at a mill where the work force is out on strike.

throstle   invented in 1814 to spin filling yarn by using a U-shaped tube of steel or double flyer which rotates around the bobbin giving twist to the yarn.

warp   yarn strengthened by the application of size or starch and which runs length-wise in woven fabric.

warper   the arranger of warp yarns into a horizontal sheet of yarn ready to be sized.

yellow-dog contract a contractual agreement between an individual employee and management which makes union activity or membership grounds for dismissal.

NOTES ON THE SOURCES

"Introduction." Information on the 1859 strike was based on Dublin, *Women At Work*, pp. 203-205. The quotation from Alice Swanton was taken from Marc Miller, "Working Women and World War II," *New England Quarterly*, LIII No. 1 (March, 1980), p. 54.

"The Lowell Mule Spinners' Strike of 1875" was based on research in the *Lowell Daily Courier* and Herbert J. Lahne, *The Cotton Millworker*, 1944.

"Tramps and Unemployed Vagrants in the Depression of the Nineties" was based on newspaper research in the *Lowell Sun*, the *Lowell Evening Mail*, the *Lowell Evening Star*, and the *Lowell Morning Times*.

"The Poor and the City Farm: Municipal Attitudes Toward Poverty" was based on research conducted by Kathy Powers Gawlik in 1975 and on a seminar paper which Gawlik wrote under the direction of Mary Blewett, "Lowell's Poor and the City Farm, 1880-1903." The sources used were the *Annual Reports of the Board of the Overseers of the Poor*, the *Reports of the Ministry-at-Large*, and the *Reports of the City Farm*.

"The 1903 Strike in the Lowell Cotton Mills" was based on research in the *Lowell Courier*, the *Lowell Sun* and *L'Etoile*. Also used were George Kennan, "The Strike in the Lowell Cotton Mills," *The Outlook* (May 30, 1903), Frederick F. Coburn, *History of Lowell and Its People*, 1920, and Herbert Lahne, *The Cotton Mill Worker*, 1944.

"Greek Workers in the Mills of Lowell" was based on interviews with Spiros Los and Costas Liacopolous in 1973 and research in the *Lowell Sun*, and the *Lowell Courier-Citizen*. Also used were Frederick F. Coburn, *History of Lowell and Its People*, 1920, and George F. Kenngott, *The Record of a City: A Social Survey of Lowell, Massachusetts*, 1912.

"Epilogue to Lawrence: The 1912 Strike in Lowell" was based on research in the *Lowell Sun*, the *Lowell Courier-Citizen*, *L'Etoile* and in the *Lawrence Sun*, the *Lawrence Telegram*, the *Lawrence Evening Tribune*, and the *Lawrence Daily American*. Other sources used include: Thomas Burgess, *Greeks in America*, 1913; Frederick F. Coburn, *History of Lowell and Its People*, 1920; Melvyn Dubofsky,

We Shall Be All: A History of the Industrial Workers of the World,
1969; George F. Kenngott, *The Record of a City: A Social Survey of
Lowell, Massachusetts,* 1912; and Herbert Lahne, *The Cotton Mill
Worker,* 1944.

"World War I and the 1918 Cotton Textile Strike" was based on
research in the *Lowell Courier-Citizen,* and the *Lowell Sun.* Other
sources were: Frederick F. Coburn, *History of Lowell and its People,*
1920; Paul Douglas, *Real Wages in the United States, 1890-1926,*
1930; Herbert Lahne, *The Cotton Mill Worker,* 1944; Philip Taft,
Organized Labor in American History, 1964; and James Weinstein,
The Corporate Ideal in the Liberal State, 1968.

"The Lowell Shoe Strike in 1933" was based on the report of the
Massachusetts Board of Conciliation and Arbitration in 1933, on
the *Lowell Courier-Citizen,* the *Lowell Evening Leader,* the *Lowell Sun*
and the *Lowell Sunday Telegram,* and on an interview in 1976 with
Richard Wright of Lowell, organizer for the SWPU in 1933.

"Yvonne Hoar: Mill Worker, Union Organizer, Shop Steward"
This interview was conducted in 1974.

"James Ellis: Mill Worker, Business Agent, CIO Organizer" This
interview was conducted in 1974.

"The Family History of Sophie and Theresa" is based on the experiences of several Lowell families.